Thanks For The Memories

Thanks For The Memories

FOR A FRIEND I CAN'T FORGET

by PERRY TANKSLEY

𝕬𝖑𝖑𝖌𝖔𝖔𝖉 𝕭𝖔𝖔𝖐𝖘

BOX 1329
JACKSON, MISSISSIPPI 39205

"As brothers we pursued rainbows
When we wern't very old,
For we thought at the foot of it
We'd find a pot of gold.
Of course, we never found it
But found the deeper pleasure
Of comradeship with brothers
Worth more than fabled treasure." *

* In this volume all quotes are borrowed and all poetry and prose have been composed by Perry Tanksley.

Thanks For The Memories

As an actor and orator, he stood reciting verse,
And the applause of the audience almost made the walls to burst.
When he asked for requested poems, one spoke in accents calm,
"Could you quote Psalm 23? I call it the Shepherd's Psalm."
The artist scornfully replied, "I'll tell you what I'll do,
I'll say it if you'll do likewise, when I have gotten through."
The grey-haired man agreed to try as the great artist stood
And repeated those verses with skill, as well as any could.
With precision of word and diction he quoted each verse to them
So flawlessly the people stood and clapped loudly for him.
Of course he felt great pride in skill displayed that day,
While far in the back of the hall stood a man stooped and grey.
Keeping the promise he had made he walked forward very slow,
And then he started to quoting with a voice shaky and low.
Finally when the psalm was finished, their thoughts were turned within;
Hearts broke, eyes wept and heads bowed as some confessed their sins.
But not a person stood up though many paused to pray,
And not one hand applauded him who was so old and grey.
The young artist left the stage so touched that tears poured down his cheek;
He came and stood by the old man in search of words to speak.
"I said the Shepherd's Psalm," he wept, "And you applauded me,
But when he said the same, I wept, and wanted to bow my knee.
You see, I knew the Shepherd's Psalm, I guess that's all I knew;
I reached your minds, he touched our hearts. He knows the Shepherd, too.

The Twenty-Third Psalm

The Lord is my shepherd; I shall not want.

He maketh me to lie down in green pastures: he leadeth me beside the still waters.

He restoreth my soul: he leadeth me in the paths of righteousness for his name's sake.

Yea, though I walk through the valley of the shadow of death, I will fear no evil: for thou art with me; thy rod and thy staff they comfort me.

Thou preparest a table before me in the presence of mine enemies: thou anointest my head with oil; my cup runneth over.

Surely goodness and mercy shall follow me all the days of my life: and I will dwell in the house of the Lord for ever.

ANYONE refusing to walk through the gate into a sheepfold, who sneaks over the wall, must surely be a thief!

2 For a shepherd comes through the gate.

3 The gatekeeper opens the gate for him, and the sheep hear his voice and come to him; and he calls his own sheep by name and leads them out.

4 He walks ahead of them; and they follow him, for they recognize his voice.

5 They won't follow a stranger but will run from him, for they don't recognize his voice. JOHN 10:1-5

11 I am the Good Shepherd. The Good Shepherd lays down His life for the sheep.

12 A hired man will run when he sees a wolf coming and will leave the sheep, for they aren't his and he isn't their shepherd. And so the wolf leaps on them and scatters the flock.

13 The hired man runs because he is hired and has no real concern for the sheep.

14 I am the Good Shepherd and know My own sheep, and they know Me,

15 Just as My Father knows Me and I know the Father, and I lay down My life for the sheep.

16 I have other sheep, too, in another fold. I must bring them also, and they will heed My voice; and there will be one flock with one Shepherd. JOHN 10:11-16

27 My sheep recognize My voice, and I know them, and they follow Me.

28 I give them eternal life and they shall never perish. No one shall snatch them away from Me,

29 For My Father has given them to Me, and He is more powerful than anyone else, so no one can kidnap them from Me. JOHN 10:27-29 *

* Biblical references in this volume are taken from Ken Taylor's *The Living New Testament: Reach Out* © 1967 and © 1969 and used by permission of Tyndale House Publishers, Wheaton, Illinois.

THE LORD IS MY SHEPHERD

A Good Shepherd Speaks . . .

To be a shepherd here in rugged Judea is a difficult and dangerous task. Yet the romance and adventure of this vocation cannot be conveyed in words. The challenge of such a demanding calling influenced me as a boy to decide to become a shepherd. I entered this task knowing full well the lonely and solitary existence a shepherd leads. To remain a shepherd demands patience and determination mingled with loyalty and love. Only another shepherd can fully grasp the deep love I feel for my flock. Often I have risked my life to save a defenseless lamb and, if necessity demanded it, I would gladly give my life to defend by sheep. I not only know each sheep by name but I am so familiar with each one's features that I, on the blackest night, can feel their faces and identify each one by name. To be a good shepherd one needs a shepherd's heart. I think I possess one. When some of us risk our lives for such helpless creatures, hired shepherds laugh at us for they know nothing of a shepherd's love. They work for their wages and place little value on the worth of a lamb or a sheep. When personal safety is involved, hirelings flee from danger, often deserting the flock to the foe. I, who claim these sheep as my very own, love them so dearly that my dangerous task seems like romance. Truly, mine is a relationship of love.

INSTEAD OF WHAT I AM

If I had been a shepherd
With little lambs to keep
I would have known the love
A shepherd has for sheep.
For shepherds sense the needs
Of wayward sheep and lame
And from the love they share
They learn each one by name.
If I had been a shepherd
Instead of what I am
I'd know the love and fondness
A shepherd has for lambs.*

* In my treatment of the 23rd Psalm I write as if I were a Judean
shepherd in biblical times. As a reader you, like the Psalmist, must let
your memory and imagination perform its task. As you read, ask yourself,
"How is the shepherd like my Lord? How am I like a sheep in the Good
Shepherd's fold?" Let every reader make his own application as Jesus
leads all into greener pastures of spiritual reality.—PERRY TANKSLEY

A SHEEP SPEAKS

My shepherd posseses me
And I'm one of his sheep;
He guides me through the day
And guards me when I sleep.
He holds me when I'm hurt
And claims me for his own,
And lest I be deserted
He leaves me not alone.
My shepherd loves me so
He leads me every day
And finds me when I'm lost
And guides me lest I stray.

I SHALL NOT WANT

A Good Shepherd Speaks . . .

In this barren and rocky land where men and animals perish with thirst and hunger, I try to keep my flock from thirst and want. Limited rainfall plus unfertile soil compound our problem and keep every diligent shepherd fearful he may fail to provide for his flock. So far, by diligence, determination, faith and sacrifice I have succeeded, not in providing over-abundance, but necessities for my sheep. My sheep of course must daily follow me if their wants are satisfied. That means treading rocky paths, steep inclines, barren deserts, shady valleys and parched pastures. Always, and almost like a miracle, I've found green pastures just when most needed. What a challenge to go forth leading innocent sheep, believing enough water and food will be found for nearly a hundred thirsty and starving creatures. Of course the hired shepherds complain of the ceaseless search and such uncaring and uncompassionate men are untouched by the plight of unsatisfied sheep. I rejoice in the attempt to be a good shepherd and am seldom discouraged by the endless quest. Often at dusk with my well-fed sheep safe in the fold, I recall how another unpromising day has turned into a great victory. Then I fall asleep dreaming of yet another day when I must lead my flock with the same faith I led them today.

And what pity He felt for the crowds that came, because their problems were so great and they didn't know what to do or where to go for help. They were like sheep without a shepherd. MATTHEW 9:36

A SHEEP SPEAKS

My shepherd cares for me
Enough to clothe and feed,
And I shall never want;
He will supply my need.
I shall not want good things
As I march toward my goal;
Yet things not good for me
I know he must withhold.
Nor shall I ever want
But if denied I know
It is for my own good
Because he loves me so.

And it is He who will supply all your needs from His riches in glory, because of what Christ Jesus has done for us.
PHILIPPIANS 4:19

LIE DOWN IN GREEN PASTURES

A Good Shepherd Speaks . . .

What a thrill for me to see my contented flock at noon-day lying down in green pastures. Such a scene bespeaks of abundance and satisfaction and growth. Of course, I know and every shepherd knows that sheep do not and cannot lie down hungry. They stalk the fold at night and during the day they wander about nervously nibbling at every sprig of grass. The heartbreak of my life has been those times when it seemed like my searching for green pastures was vain. My proudest moments have been those instances when I have searched and found abundant provisions so that my flock could rest serenely in green pastures of plenty. That singular reward daily prods me forward until my foremost concern is knowing where good pastures are, where streams and springs flow and most of all to know the nearest and safest path. The hardships of such a quest cause hired shepherds to give up if the way is too difficult. Even if the sheep go unfed and cannot sleep because of hunger, the hireling enjoys his food and sleeps soundly. I am so hurt by bleating sheep that I cannot rest if they are restless. Food sticks in my throat if I know they are hungry. In a sense I bear in my body the sufferings of my sheep. I suffer their hungers, thirsts, anxieties, and tiredness. I also taste deeply of the happiness and contentment they experience.

Like sheep you wandered away from God, but now you have returned to your Shepherd, the Guardian of your souls who keeps you safe from all attacks. I PETER 2:25

A SHEEP SPEAKS

With love my shepherd makes
Me lie in pastures green
And I view landscapes gleaming
Such as are seldom seen.
With plenty so abounding
My shepherd kneels to soothe
Sheep weary from the journey
On steep paths so unsmooth.
So satisfied am I
With love the shepherd shares
That I would always tarry
In pastures he prepares.

Let heaven fill your thoughts; don't spend your time worrying about things down here. COLOSSIANS 3:2

BESIDE THE STILL WATERS

A Good Shepherd Speaks . . .

Here in this parched land the most precious commodity of all is refreshing water. During the three month rainy season, creek banks and river banks overflow but during the nine month drought that follows, the rushing streams are reduced to a trickle and most of the creeks dry up completely. Every wise shepherd takes advantage of the rainy season storing up water in cisterns, pools, vats and ponds which he arranges for. Of course he has to build such storage places close to streams so that during the wet season he can divert water into them. Often he must secretly conceal his storage places lest unfriendly shepherds take advantage of his labor. I take large slabs of rock and place across the entrance of my cisterns and vats. Sometimes I place brush or grass on these to further conceal. Actually there is no other way to water my flock than that I should store up water for the lengthy dry season. In many pastures and beside many a dried-up stream I have secret cisterns of water. As I daily lead my flock in search of grazing land I am strengthened by the knowledge that in a thirsty land I have provided so well for my sheep. The water is always cool and clear and still. Actually sheep will not drink from a rushing stream so the still water of a vat or pool is appropriate at midday in the midst of a burning desert. How I love to lead my sheep to the secret water holes I've provided!

And now beware! Be sure that you feed and shepherd God's flock—His church, purchased with His blood—for the Holy Spirit is holding you responsible as overseers.

I know full well that after I leave you, false teachers, like vicious wolves, will appear among you, not sparing the flock. ACTS 20:28-29

A SHEEP SPEAKS

He leads my feet beside
Still waters fresh and cool;
Shepherds know sheep cannot
Drink from a rushing pool.
Contented by still waters
Until night shades are drawn
I know I'll never thirst
And so he leads me on.
He leads but never drives
For kindness is his rule
And so I follow Him
To waters still and cool.

For the earth and every good thing in it belongs to the Lord and is yours to enjoy. I CORINTHIANS 10:26

HE RESTORETH MY SOUL

A Good Shepherd Speaks . . .

Most animals possess a fine sense of direction. No animal known to man possesses a poorer sense of direction than sheep. Without the homing instinct, sheep are often lost, wandering aimlessly in search of greener pastures. They seem stupidly unaware of danger, often venturing where devouring enemies lurk. Wild animals often pounce upon lost sheep and unscruplous robbers dig horrible pits for straying sheep to be trapped into. Here in this hostile land many rocky ledges overhanging deadly ravines threaten sheep that wander from the flock. The only safety for a sheep is in the flock and following the shepherd. Unfriendly shepherds can claim a straying sheep should it wander on to his pastures. To make the problem more acute, sheep have very poor vision, seeing only fifty yards away. Because of all these factors I have unusual concern for the safety of my flock. I keep constant watch over them and often recount them. Should I discover one missing I lead my flock down the path we've just travelled and as I double back I race into the side paths and look into the ravines. To find a straying sheep is an unforgettable experience of indescribable joy. To rescue a frightened lamb from a deep gulch and place its trembling body upon ones shoulders and to restore it to the flock is a shepherd's highest joy. Restoring my wandering sheep I have known that joy.

Feed the flock of God; care for it willingly, not grudgingly; not for what you will get out of it, but because you are eager to serve the Lord.

Don't be tyrants, but lead them by your good example,

And when the Head Shepherd comes, your reward will be a never-ending share in His glory and honor. II PETER 5:2-4

A SHEEP SPEAKS

Oft searching through the shadows,
More oft in light of day
A shepherd brokenhearted
Seeks every sheep astray.
And when I wander far
My shepherd calls my name,
And when he finds me trembling
I'm always glad he came.
And finding me lest I
Should perish unrestored
He shouts for joy and then
His love on me outpours.

You know how full of love and kindness our Lord Jesus was: though He was so very rich, yet to help you He became so very poor, so that by being poor He could make you rich.

II CORINTHIANS 8:9

17

IN PATHS OF RIGHTEOUSNESS

A Good Shepherd Speaks . . .

To be known as a faithful shepherd is my one ambition. Such a proud possession is mine and to keep such a reputation is my objective. For that reason I cannot mistakenly lead my flock down dangerous paths where needless chances are taken. Only a foolish shepherd would needlessly lead his flock along a narrow ledge where death invites. Such a lack of foresight on the part of hireling shepherds have resulted in tragedy untold. This rocky land is filled with traps and precipices which keep me on my toes lest I lead my flock astray. In less dangerous lands shepherds drive their flocks and the sheep go before. Here, we shepherds go before the sheep checking out dangers, avoiding pits, bypassing precipices and in a sense risking our lives for the sheep. Always we are aware that sheep have little concern for their safety and are mostly unaware of danger. For that reason I as a responsible and dedicated shepherd have learned to make every decision in light of what is best for my sheep. When paths cross and I have to decide, the overriding concern of my mind is this: what path will benefit my flock most. Choosing the right path and leading them confidently is a big part of my task. Because I have never betrayed them they follow me unafraid.

For when He punishes you, it proves that He loves you.
When He whips you it proves you are really His child."
HEBREWS 12:6

A SHEEP SPEAKS

He knows what's best for me
And when I'm called to go
He'll lead me down good paths,
That's why I trust him so.
I follow him assured
Though tears oft blind my sight
That my good shepherd cares
Enough to guide aright.
Then I will follow him
Believing he will bless
And ever lead me on
In paths of righteousness.

If the Good News we preach is hidden to anyone, it is hidden
from the one who is on the road to eternal death.
II CORINTHIANS 4:3

I WALK THROUGH
THE VALLEY

A Good Shepherd Speaks . . .

Judea, a land of many mountains, is likewise a land of many valleys. These valleys are passageways between the mountains. Often the passageway is a narrow path bordered on both sides by rocky cliffs soaring hundreds of feet above. Sometimes the way through the valley is a ledge on the side of a mountain with an abyss on the other side. One such abyss here bordering a valley path drops six hundred feet. Except at midday, the sun seldom shines on such a passageway. Such gloomy paths bordered by such perpendicular cliffs become a valley of shadows. Because such an eerie passage lurks with hidden foes, it becomes for some the valley of death. Ruthless robbers hide in the caves victimizing travellers as well as sheep. Starving animals stalk the shadowy corridor anxious to pounce upon frightened sheep. I, as a Judean shepherd, know to avoid these places of shadows but should necessity demand I venture through leading my flock, I would not go unprepared. Going before my sheep I would make sure it was safe to follow. Lest my flock be attacked from the rear and panic over some ledge, I would take special protective measures. I have successfully led my flock, on needy occasions, through dangerous valleys in search of greener pastures. To emerge from the valley of shadows into the sunshine of safety is an incomparable experience.

No, for the Scriptures tell us that for His sake we must be ready to face death at every moment of the day—we are like sheep awaiting slaughter;

But despite all this, overwhelming victory is ours through Christ who loved us enough to die for us. ROMANS 8:36-37

A SHEEP SPEAKS

Through valleys bleak with shadows
Where strength and courage waste
My shepherd sometimes asks
I follow him with faith.   3 ems
And though I fear dark shadows
Yet still I follow him
Believing he'll lead me
Through valleys grey and grim.
Let me fear not dark valleys
For when the shadows flee
I'll sing in sunlit pastures
Of him who walked with me.

We know that the same God who brought the Lord Jesus back from death will also bring us back to life again with Jesus, and present us to Him along with you. II CORINTHIANS 4:14

THY ROD AND THY STAFF

A Good Shepherd Speaks . . .

In this threatened and hostile land every shepherd carries at least two weapons with him. My rod is actually a club about two feet long with a nob on one end. It is actually a deadly weapon with sharp iron spikes protruding from the nob. Such a weapon is never used on sheep but I would use this cudgel against man or beast which threatens the safety of my beloved flock. Attached to the opposite end of my rod is a leather noose which also attaches to my belt when my rod is not in use. In combat I thrust my hand through the noose lest I drop my weapon. Another weapon I use which is more like a tool is my staff. It is a slender pole about six feet in length, usually straight, but sometimes has a crook in one end. I use my staff to discipline my sheep. I never strike them with unreasonable anger or with the intention of destroying. Actually I spank my wayward and disobedient sheep to teach them obedience. Such is not for my pleasure but their good. In fact it pains me to strike them but I know of no other way to save them from straying. Sometimes my staff helps retrieve a sheep which has fallen over a cliff and sometimes I use it to pull tree limbs and foliage down to sheep level. Always, whether they know it or not, my rod and staff comfort, preserve and save the sheep.

Let God train you, for He is doing what any loving father does for his children. Whoever heard of a son who was never corrected?

If God doesn't punish you when you need it, as other fathers punish their sons, then it means that you aren't really God's son at all—that you don't really belong in His family. HEBREWS 12:7, 8

A SHEEP SPEAKS

My shepherd's rod and staff
Keeps me in the way,
Comforting and saving me,
Should I go astray.
His rod is used to guard
Me from my foes of wrath
Who would if it were possible
Allure me from the path.
My shepherd comforts me
With rod and staff each day
And with them he'll keep me
Safe on a dangerous way.

Being punished isn't enjoyable while it is happening—it hurts! But afterwards we can see the result, a quiet growth in grace and character. HEBREWS 12:11

THOU PREPAREST A TABLE

A Good Shepherd Speaks . . .

My sheep are utterly defenseless in the presence of danger. They know nothing of defending themselves or how to ward off the enemy. Not only are wild animals the enemy of sheep but there are many deadly plants and weeds which a shepherd constantly fears and is on the lookout for. Always before entering a new pasture I halt my flock and walk over every foot of pasture, plucking noxious weeds and poisonous plants. In such pastures we look for cobra snakes which subtly wait for an opportunity to strike an intruding animal. Much more deadly than the cobra is the eighteen-inch long viper. These hide in holes and strike the nose of unsuspecting sheep. So deadly are they that their bite kills sheep in half an hour. I cover their hiding places with slabs of rocks but if I have fire with me, I pour oil in the tiny hole and set it afire. Vipers sense their predicament and try to flee the wrath of burning. As they burst out of hiding I with my rod or staff destroy them. In the lambing season evil vultures dive down and attack little lambs freshly born. In spite of the presence of all these enemies my grandest delight is to prepare a table, a pastureland, a good grazing spot for the flock I possess and dearly love. In the midst of threatening foes and in the presence of evil I feed my sheep.

Most of all, let love guide your life for then the whole church will stay together in perfect harmony.

Let the peace of heart which comes from Christ be always present in your hearts and lives, for this is your responsibility and privilege as members of His body. And always be thankful. COLOSSIANS 3:14, 15

A SHEEP SPEAKS

He spreads a table now
Though foes blight and deride,
And pastures that I graze
Are made safe by my guide.
For my good shepherd spreads
An eating place for all,
For pastures are to sheep
Their only banquet hall.
My shepherd still prepares
For sheep so plagued with blindness
A table filled with bounty,
Made safe and blessed with kindness.

So don't be afraid, little flock. For it gives your Father great happiness to give you the Kingdom. LUKE 12:32

THOU ANOINTEST MY HEAD

A Good Shepherd Speaks . . .

To a shepherd in this barren land, a day can seem very long and tiring. I, along with other shepherds, leave our village early in the morning. We proceed down a common path and when anyone wishes to turn aside, he calls his sheep out of the larger flock and they, recognizing his voice, follow him. By mid-afternoon I am usually quite weary and so are my sheep. Because the return may consume several hours I head for the village as the evening shadows begin to lengthen. Other weary shepherds join me as our flocks once again mingle together. Sheep have a wonderful ear for identifying their shepherds voice so when I step aside and call mine out to lead them back to their fold, they obey and follow. My fold is a square, unroofed, fort-like enclosure with one narrow entrance through the ten-feet high walls. Each night, until I've passed upon a sheep's physical condition he cannot enter the fold for I stand in the door. Actually there is no door and as I stand in the opening, which is the width of my shoulders, I prevent them entering. When I've removed briars from festering feet, checked each sheep and lamb for fever and poured healing oil upon each bruised head and grazed body I, like a door, turn aside and admit the weary sheep. I become so thoroughly familiar with their ills and fevers that I can and do call each one by name. Except they enter the sheepfold by me they cannot enter at all. If any enters any other way he is a thief. Such climb over the barricades at night with the purpose of destroying the sheep. On the top edge of my fold I have woven together strands of thorns and briars with the purpose of keeping robbers out.

Then He saved us—not because we were good enough to
be saved, but because of His kindness and pity—by washing
away our sins and giving us the new joy of the indwelling Holy
Spirit.

Whom He poured out upon us with wonderful fullness—
and all because of what Jesus Christ our Savior did.

TITUS 3:5-6

A SHEEP SPEAKS

Upon my head oft bruised
The shepherd's oil of healing
Pours freely from his cup
And soon I'm better feeling.
His healing balm out poured
So soothes my weary heart
That I, feverish from tiredness,
Find all my pains depart.
With love my friend anoints
My heart and anguished head
Admitting me at evening
Into my fold and bed.

Let your roots grow down into Him and draw up nourish-
ment from Him. See that you go on growing in the Lord, and
become strong and vigorous in the truth. Let your lives overflow
with joy and thanksgiving for all He has done. COLOSSIANS 2:7

MY CUP RUNNETH OVER

A Good Shepherd Speaks . . .

Here in Judea shepherds erect their sheepfolds as near to a stream as possible. Even in the driest months the stream must produce a trickle if a hundred thirsty sheep are watered. While I'm leading my flock in search of food, members of my family channel enough water from the stream to overflow two large iron cups. Sometimes my sheep drink from these cups while they are sitting beside the stream. Usually my sheep upon entering the fold discover overflowing cups of refreshing water. Even while I sleep I have ways of capturing fresh water so my sheep will have their thirst quenched before they depart from the fold. That I can provide for so large a flock in such a drought-stricken land is little short of miracelous. When I have examined each sheep, anointed the bruised ones with oil, and turned to let the last one enter, I then turn to the task of building a fire several yards away from the single entrance. Then I eat my simple fare and lie down across the entrance lest animals or men intrude. Warmed by the fire and wearied from my labor I fall asleep, knowing the ten-foot high walls will keep my sheep safe. The robber may come to destroy but first he must go over my body. I feel no man can pluck these sheep out of my hand. The fire not only warms me through the chill of a Judean night but best of all keeps blood-thirsty devourers away. Should I discover at the end of a day that one of my sheep is missing I would get a member of my household to watch over my flock while I went in search. To retrace your steps and search all night is worth it all when you find at last a confused and wandering sheep.

When I think of the wisdom and scope of His plan I fall down on my knees and pray to the Father of all the great family of God—some of them already in heaven and some down here on earth—

That out of His glorious, unlimited resources He will give you the mighty inner strengthening of His Holy Spirit.

EPHESIANS 3:14-16

A SHEEP SPEAKS

My shepherd makes his blessings
Overflow my cup,
And I, athirst, keep drinking
And it keeps filling up.
At eve my cup o'er flows
And soaks into the sod
For in this land of drought
There's plenty where I trod.
Let every thirsty one
Who feels like giving up
Learn that my shepherd gives
An over-brimming cup.

And I pray that Christ will be more and more at home in your hearts, living within you as you trust in Him. May your roots go down deep into the soil of God's marvelous love. . . .
EPHESIANS 3:17

GOODNESS AND MERCY
FOLLOW

A Good Shepherd Speaks . . .

My success as a shepherd depends upon one factor seldom mentioned. As I lead my flock I have two loyal dogs bringing up the rear. Without them, wild animals or evil men could surprise me and plunder my flock. Their warning bark alerts me to any danger threatening. My flock stays together because my well-trained dogs hound the heels of any straggling or straying sheep. My dogs following my sheep, keeping them together, driving them closer to the shepherd, and forcing them to go forward, are a type of disguised goodness and mercy. Of course my unthinking sheep hardly think of the dogs as conveyors of mercy or harbingers of goodness. They're only aware that vigilant dogs bark at their heels and hound their steps when they stray. Perhaps on rare occasion these dumb but loveable creatures fully sense their security is directly related to that which drives them as I lead. I doubt they consider the dogs their best friends but had they a keener understanding I'm sure they would realize the worth of my dogs. It is the protective instinct of good shepherds which cause them to provide vicious dogs to guard straggling sheep. Such merciful goodness results in our safe venturing each day and in our successful return to the fold each night. I consider my dogs a vital and integral part of my success as a shepherd.

Oh, what a wonderful God we have! How great are His wisdom and knowledge and riches! How impossible it is for us to understand His decisions and His methods! ROMANS 11:33

A SHEEP SPEAKS

Surely goodness and mercy
All the days of life
Hound my steps like dogs,
Guarding me in strife.
And I am always guarded
By him who cannot fail
For goodness and mercy guard
When evil foes assail.
Then let me forward press
Through danger and disaster,
Still closer to my shepherd
And nearer to my master.

Since we respect our fathers here on earth, though they punish us, should we not all the more cheerfully submit to God's training so that we can begin to really live?

Our earthly fathers trained us for a few brief years, doing the best for us that they knew how, but God's correction is always right and for our best good, that we may share His holiness. HEBREWS 12:9, 10

I WILL DWELL IN THE HOUSE

A Good Shepherd Speaks . . .

Life for a shepherd is a constant going in and going out. I daily go out in search of new pastures and nightly I return to the fold. Every day is a new experience and I can never rest on a past days performance. The sheepfold is a resting place but is not a constant resting place. A part of the glory of a shepherd's life is the loyalty of his sheep. As a shepherd imparts love, security, and a great sense of belonging, the flock returns the love and comes to possess an even greater sense of belonging. After they have followed me through deserts, fields, valleys, and back to the fold each day, a deep loyalty toward the shepherd and toward the flock develops. That is particularly true of the shepherd who provides for the total needs of his flock. Such a perfect life for the sheep results in perfect contentment for the flock. That has been my one objective: to minister to every need so they will be proud to belong to me and always desire to remain in my fold and forever be a part of my plans. If they recognize my voice, I much more recognize each of their voices and am most anxious to help each sheep when he cries. Even with their poor vision which hinders them seeing very far, yet they know my voice and they follow unafraid. I'll never forsake them and being loved as they are I can well understand why they would like to remain in my care forever.

For this world is not our home; we are looking forward to our everlasting home in heaven. HEBREWS 13:14

A SHEEP SPEAKS

At night the sheepfold beckons.
My shepherd is the door.
He turns and I go in
Where oft I've gone before.
But morning comes renewed
And I, waked by my master,
Go forth to follow him
Who leads to greener pastures.
I'll follow him always
In hope that nothing severs
Me from my shepherd's fold.
I'll dwell with him forever.

May our Lord Jesus Christ Himself and God our Father, who has loved us and given us everlasting comfort and hope which we don't deserve,

Comfort your hearts with all comfort, and help you in every good thing you say and do. II THESSALONIANS 2:16, 17

IS HE MY SHEPHERD

Do I know the Lord Jesus Christ as my shepherd who said, "I am the good shepherd. The good shepherd lays down his life for the sheep." John 10:11,12

Do I know the Christ and most of all am I known of Him who said, "I am the good shepherd; I know my own and my own know me." John 10:14

Have I entered the sheepfold through the Lord Jesus Christ who said, "Truly, truly, I say to you, he who does not enter the sheepfold by the door but climbs in by another way, that man is a thief and a robber; but he who enters by the door is the shepherd of the sheep." John 10:1–2

Do I always follow my shepherd, the Lord Jesus, who said, "He calls his own sheep by name and leads them out. When he has brought out all his own, he goes before them, and the sheep follow him, for they know his voice." John 10:3–4

Do I realize the security offered by my Good Shepherd who said, "My sheep hear my voice, and I know them, and they follow me; and I give them eternal life, and they shall never perish, and no one shall snatch them out of my hand." John 10:27,28 Do I really realize that the Good Shepherd guards me lest I perish or am snatched from Christ?

Do I sense the safety of the fold of my Master who taught, "My Father, who has given them to me, is greater than all, and no one is able to snatch them out of the Father's hand." John 10:29

Have I found abundance and satisfaction in following my shepherd who said, "I am the door; if any one enters by me, he will be saved, and will go in and out and find pasture. The thief comes only to steal and kill and destroy; I came that they may have life, and have it abundantly." John 10:9–10

Do I realize how much He loves me who said, "I lay down my life that I may take it again. No one takes it from me, but I lay it down of my own accord."

And now may the God of peace who brought again from the dead our Lord Jesus, the great Shepherd of the sheep, equip you with all you need for doing His will, through the blood of the everlasting agreement between God and you.

HEBREWS 13:20

HE FEELS OUR FACE

At night a shepherd knows
Each lamb and sheep that's his;
In dark he feels each face
And knows which one it is.
Good shepherds know each sheep
And answers every need,
And not one lamb can cry
But that he quickly heeds.
And so familiar is
My Shepherd with each lamb
That on the darkest night
Christ knows just who I am.

And may He produce in you through the power of Christ all that is pleasing to Him, to whom be glory forever and ever. Amen. HEBREWS 13:21

BUILDING MONUMENTS

Harsh critics threw their stones
And I resented it,
But I knew in my heart
That I could not prevent it.
'Twas then insight was granted
And I used rocks they flung
As blessings in disguise,
As they had been for some.
Some rocks were stepping stones
And others hurled in blindness
I dared pile high and build
A monument to kindness.

SERF-TASKS TRANSFORMED

The greatness of my Master
Was that while on the earth
He did such common things,
And doing them found mirth.
He laughed with little children
And smiled at friendless faces,
And touched the down-and-outers
In out-of-the-way places.
Among the poor and lonely
And far from greater things
He turned serf-tasks into
Work worthy of a king.

It is magnificent to grow old if one keeps young.—*
HARRY EMERSON FOSDICK

We never stop laughing because we are old. We grow old because we stop laughing.

When you begin to notice what a jolly time the young people are having, you're getting old.

Anyone who stops learning is old whether this happens at twenty or eighty. Anyone who keeps on learning not only remains young but becomes increasingly valuable.

The best thing for grey hair is a sensible head.

When saving for old age, be sure to lay up a few pleasant thoughts.

AGREEMENT

My idea of an agreeable person is a person who agrees with me.—DISRAELI

A well-informed person is one who has opinions just like ours.

APOLOGY

A man should never be ashamed to say he has been wrong, which is but saying in other words that he is wiser today than he was yesterday.—
ALEXANDER POPE

---

* All quotes in this volume have been borrowed from dozens of sources. Credit is given when possible. Prose and poetry in this volume have been composed by Perry Tanksley.

AMERICA

The true test of civilization is not the census nor the size of cities or crops but the kind of man the country turns out.—RALPH WALDO EMERSON

ARGUMENT

You can't prove anything in an argument, except that you're just as bull-headed as the other fellow.

ACHIEVEMENT

Unless a man undertakes more than he possibly can do, he will never do all that he can.—HENRY DRUMMOND

ACCOMPLISHMENT

You can get anything done if you don't care who gets the credit.

ADVERSITY

The purpose of the tests of life are to make, not break us.—MALTBIE BABCOCK

God had one Son on earth without sin, but never one without suffering.—ST. AUGUSTINE

It lightens the stroke to draw near to Him who handles the rod.—TRYON EDWARDS

ATHEIST

An atheist cannot find God for the same reason a thief cannot find a policeman.

ANXIETY

What does your anxiety do? It does not empty tomorrow of its sorrow; but ah! it empties today of its strength. It does not make you escape the evil; it makes you unfit to cope with it if it comes.—IAN MACLAREN

BURDENS

Life is a procession of people bearing crosses and when one carries his awkwardly he interferes with his fellow marchers.—R. C. McCARTHY

The Bible says to bear one anothers burden, not to bear down on them.

A heavy weight is necessary to keep the diver down while he is hunting pearls. The burden God gives also results in discovering rare and costly pearls of wisdom and patience.

BRAVERY

Learning to cover up an aching heart, to smile when you would weep, is what everyone must learn if he would live the masterful life.

BROTHERHOOD

The man who walks humbly with his God is not likely to run over his fellow man.

The world is now too dangerous for anything but the truth and too small for anything but brotherhood.
—ARTHUR POWELL DAVIS

The secret of brotherhood is found in a common nearness to the Lord.—JOHN HENRY JOWETT

Christians may not see eye to eye but they can walk arm in arm.

BETRAYAL

An empty tomb proves Christianity but an empty Church denies it.

BACKSLIDING

If nine-tenths of you were as weak physically as you are spiritually, you couldn't walk.—BILLY SUNDAY

Life's greatest tragedy is to lose God and not miss Him.

BELIEF

When belief moves in the direction of truth, it won't be long in reaching certainty.

BEAUTY

If you wisely invest in beauty it will remain with you through life.—FRANK LLOYD WRIGHT

Never lose an opportunity to see anything beautiful. Beauty is God's handwriting.—CHARLES KINGSLEY

The most consummately beautiful thing in the universe is the rightly fashioned life of a good person. —GEORGE H. PALMER

Beauty at sixteen is natures gift; at sixty it is the soul's own doing.

40

BLESSINGS

Thou who hast given us so much, mercifully grant us one thing more—a grateful heart.—George Herbert

Don't stop with counting your blessings; think also of the misfortunes which you may have had but didn't.

BIBLE

While I can't understand parts of the Bible there are other parts I can't misunderstand.

Critics swear the Bible contradicts itself when actually it contradicts their deeds.

BENEVOLENCE

There cannot be a more glorious object in creation than a human being replete with benevolence, meditating in what manner he may render himself most acceptable to the Creator by doing good to his creatures.—Henry Fielding

BOOKS

Those who don't read good books have no advantage over those who can't read them.

BIRTH

No man is high-born until he is born from on high.

BABY

A baby is the little rivet in the bonds of matrimony.

BOREDOM

There are those who pray for eternal life who don't know how to use a rainy afternoon.

Christianity is not a human speculation about God; it is a divine revelation to man.

Some people use Christianity like a bus; they ride on it only when it is going their way.

Is your Christianity ancient history or current events? —SAMUEL SHOEMAKER

Christianity is not a puzzle to be solved, but a Way of life to be adopted. It is not a creed to be memorized but a Person to follow.

The acid test of our orthodoxy is not the accuracy of our opinions, but the graciousness of our lives. Christians down through the centuries have not distinguished themselves for their philosophy but for their gentleness. To fail in gentility, good humor, goodwill, charity, dependability and kindliness is to betray our Lord even though we proclaim our belief in all the fundamentals.—ROY L. SMITH

There is no argument for Christianity like Christ and there is no defense and confirmation of the gospel like a Christian. Give me but one—if there is but one Christian in the world—and I will prove the gospel by him.—HENRY G. WESTON

CONSCIENCE

Before our conscience punishes us as a judge, it warns us as a friend.—STANISLUS

CHILDREN

The church which neglects the children will have children who neglect the church.

We receive love from our children as well as others —not in proportion to our demands or sacrifice or needs, but roughly in proportion to our capacity to love.—Rollo May

What the best and wisest parent wants for his own child, that must the community want for all its children.—John Dewey

I have often thought what a melancholy world this would be without children, and what an inhuman world without the aged.—Samuel Taylor Coleridge

Children may tear up a house but they can never break up a home.

Children need love especially when they do not deserve it.—H. S. Hulbert

The most influential of all educational factors is the conversation in a child's home.—William Temple

If you make children happy now, you will make them happy twenty years hence by the memory of it.— Kate Douglas Wiggin

I love little children and it is not a slight thing when they, who are fresh from God, love us.—Charles Dickens

A torn jacket is soon mended, but harsh words bruise the heart of a child.—Henry W. Longfellow

CHURCH

The man who is not proud of his church seldom makes the church proud of him.

The church is not an art gallery for exhibition of eminent Christians, but a school for the education of imperfect ones.—HENRY WARD BEECHER

It is better to build a fence around the top of the precipice before the child goes over it than it is to build a hospital at the bottom of it.—GYPSY SMITH

The church has suffered from putting too high a premium on orthodoxy in words and too little emphasis upon superiority in deeds and character.

The first steps of happiness are the church steps.

CONVERSION

Conversion is the process, gradual or sudden, by which a self hitherto divided and consciously wrong and unhappy becomes unified and consciously right and happy in consequence of its firmer hold on religious realities.—WILLIAM JAMES

CHARITY

The greatest difficulty with the world is not its inability to produce, but its unwillingness to share.—ROY L. SMITH

I have tried to keep things in my hands and lost them all, but what I have given into God's hands I still possess.—MARTIN LUTHER

Posthumous charities are the very essence of selfishness when bequeathed by those who, while alive, would part with nothing.—C. C. COLTON

Charity eases the conscience of the rich more often than it eases the condition of the poor.

The Christian is not one who has gone all the way with Christ. None of us has. The Christian is one who has found the right road.—CHARLES L. ALLEN

Some Christians are like porcupines. They have many fine points but its hard to get next to them. —VANCE HAVNER

A Christian is one who knows how to acquire without cheating, how to lose without regret, and how to give without hesitation.

Christians seldom choose between good or bad. We daily choose between good or best.

A Christian should not be a question mark for God, but an exclamation point.—VANCE HAVNER

CHARACTER

Learn to say 'No!' It will be of more use to you than to be able to read Latin.—CHARLES SPURGEON

CREED

My creed is spoken by my life, not my lips.

CHURCH-GOING

Church-going is not the essence of religion, but it is the evidence.

DISCIPLINE

Whether you like it or not, read and pray daily. It is for your life; there is no other way, else you will be a trifler all your days. Do justice to your own soul; give it time and means to grow. Do not starve yourself any longer.—JOHN WESLEY

How a boy turns out is often the result of when a boy turns in.

Certain bright children need to be briskly applauded with one hand while their face is turned.

Children seldom step on the toes of parents who put their feet down firmly.

DIVORCE

The only thing one can expect from divorce is a different set of problems to work with, or the old ones in a new setting.—L. A. KIRKENDALL

Divorce means simply that democracy has failed to work between two people.

Divorce usually occurs when a husband decides he's too good to be true.

DEEDS

Christianity is not believing the impossible but doing the incredible.—SHERWOOD EDDY

DISCONTENT

We are never more discontented with others than when we are discontented with ourselves.

Show me a thoroughly satisfied man and I will show you a failure.

DESTINY

Now God be thanked who has matched us with this hour!—RUPERT BROOKE

DEVOTIONS

In the secret place of my heart there is a little door which, if I open and enter, I am in the presence of God.—JOSEPH FORT NEWTON

DIFFICULTIES

Difficulties either make us better or bitter.

Difficulties are things that show what men are.— EPICTETUS

DUTY

Our grand business is not to see what lies dimly at a distance but to do what lies clearly at hand.— THOMAS CARLYLE

The reward of a thing well done is to have done it.—RALPH WALDO EMERSON

He does most in God's great world who does his best in his own little world.—THOMAS JEFFERSON

Duties are tasks we look forward to with distaste, perform with reluctance, and brag about ever after.

Let us have faith that right makes might and in that faith let us, to the end, dare to do our duty as we understand it.—A. LINCOLN

Don't waste time looking for four leaf clovers when there are weeds in your garden.

Even if I knew that tomorrow the world would go to pieces, I would still plant my apple tree.—MARTIN LUTHER

The Lord doesn't want first place in my life. He wants all of my life.—HOWARD AMERDING

I put no value on anything I possess save in terms of the Kingdom of God.

I am only one but I am one. I cannot do everything but I can do something; and what I should do and can do, by the grace of God, I will do.

DIPLOMACY

A diplomat is a man who always remembers a woman's birthday but never remembers her age.—ROBERT FROST

He who has learned to disagree without being disagreeable has discovered the most valuable secret of the diplomat.

Diplomacy is the knack of letting the other fellow have your way.

ENVIRONMENT

If your Christianity won't work where you are, it won't work anywhere.—VANCE HAVNER

EXAMPLE

If you wish your neighbors to see what God is like, let them see what he can make you like.—CHARLES KINGSLEY

Example is more forcible than precept. People look at me six days a week to see what I mean on the seventh.—RICHARD CECIL

Train up a child in the way he should go and go that way yourself.

Children are natural mimics—they act like their parents in spite of every attempt to teach them good manners.

There is just one way to bring up a child in the way he should go and that is to travel that way yourself.—A. LINCOLN

The best commentary upon the Bible is a good life.

People take your example far more seriously than they do your advice.

The world goes forward on the feet of its youth. Where those feet will lead the world is determined by what road they walk now, with us adults.—STELLA SCURLOCK

We cannot journey without leaving footprints, and others will follow where we go because we have marked the way.

ENTHUSIASM

If you can give your son only one gift, let it be enthusiasm.—BRUCE BARTON

Years wrinkle your skin but to give up enthusiasm wrinkles your soul.—SAMUEL ULLMAN

EDUCATION

A child educated only at school is an uneducated child.—SANTAYANA

The only thing more expensive than education is ignorance.

Americans spend more for gum than for books because its easier to exercise the chin than the mind.

49

The money we save on education this year will be spent later on jails and reformatories.

The world is always deciding between better schools or bigger wars.

Education is something you get when your father sends you to college but it isn't complete until you send your son there.

The best and most important part of every man's education is that which he gives himself.—Edward Gibbon

EATING

Too many square meals make too many round people.

Travelling is a broadening experience especially if you stop at all the recommended eating places along the road.

ENVY

Getting married is a good deal like going to a restaurant with your friends. You order what you want and then when you see what the other fellow got, you wish you had taken that.—Clarence Darrow

EASTER

Our Lord has written the promise of the resurrection not in books alone, but in every leaf in springtime. —Martin Luther

EXPERIENCE

To tell you something you don't know is like coming back from somewhere you haven't been.—Vance Havner

One could retire comfortably in his old age if he could sell his experience for what it cost him.

Experience is what you get while looking for something else.

The ordinary man profits by his own experience, the wise man by the other fellows.

Good judgment comes from experience and experience comes from poor judgment.

Christianity is like electricity, it cannot enter a person unless it can pass through.—RICHARD RAINES

The followers of Jesus learn not a theory so much as experience a Presence; embrace not a doctrine so much as enter a fellowship.

EXPLOITS

Most of us think we could move mountains if someone would clear the hills out of the way.

ERROR

Admission of error is a sign of strength rather than a confession of weakness.

ENCOURAGEMENT

The safest way to knock the chip off a fellow's shoulder is by patting him on the back.—FRANKLIN JONES

EVIL

It is not enough for the gardener to love flowers; he must also hate weeds.

If a man has any religion he must give it away or give it up.—BISHOP WHATLEY

EVANGELISM

Evangelism is to present Jesus Christ in the power of the Holy Spirit that men might come to trust Him as Saviour and serve Him as Lord in the fellowship of His church.—WILLIAM TEMPLE

EFFORT

God is more anxious to forgive the blotted page of endeavor than the blank page of surrender.

There is no man, no woman, so small but that they can make their lives great by high endeavor.—THOMAS CARLYLE

EXCELLENCE

The true calling of a Christian is not to do extraordinary things, but to do ordinary things in an extraordinary way.—DEAN STANLEY

ENEMIES

Speak well of your enemies. Remember, you made them.

Nobody can have too many friends but one enemy constitutes a surplus.

FAITHFULNESS

Be faithful in hard places that you may be trusted in high places.

FAITH

The beginning of anxiety is the end of faith, and the beginning of true faith is the end of anxiety.—GEORGE MUELLER

There are a thousand ways of pleasing God, but not one without faith.

Belief is a truth held in the mind. Faith is a fire in the heart.—JOSEPH FORT NEWTON

Faith is not belief without proof but trust without reservations.—ELTON TRUEBLOOD

Faith is to the soul what a mainspring is to a watch.

Those who live on mountain tops have a longer day than those who live in the valley. Then let us brighten our day rising a little higher.

The Christian faith does not consist in the belief that we are saved, but in the belief that we are loved.

Faith is dead to doubt, dumb to discouragement, and blind to impossibilities.

Christianity teaches a man to spend the best part of his life preparing for the worst.

When I cannot live by the faith of assurance I live by the faith of adherence.—MATTHEW HENRY

FANATICISM

Fanaticism is redoubling your effort when you have forgotten your aim.

It's easier to restrain a fanatic than to resurrect a corpse.

FOLLOW

To praise Christ is easy even for the cowardly. To follow Him requires courage.

FREEDOM

Only a virtuous people can be free. Freedom can survive only if the people are inwardly governed by a moral law.—JOHN COURTNEY MURRAY

Freedom is dangerous but it is still the safest form of government.

Freedom of speech is empty unless we have something to say.—ROBERT M. HUTCHINS

We have used our freedom in such a way that it seems a dangerous concept to those who have never had it, to whom it has been nothing but a word.—JOHN FOSTER DULLES

FEARS

We promise according to our hopes, and perform according to our fears.—LA ROCHEFOUCAULD

FUTURE

I am not afraid of tomorrow for I have seen yesterday and I love today.—WILLIAM ALLEN WHITE

The best thing about the future is that it only comes one day at a time.

For some reason the future arrives here sooner than it used to.

It is the business of the future to be dangerous.—ALFRED NORTH WHITEHEAD

Many are well-prepared for a rainy day who are totally unprepared for eternity.

FRUITFULNESS

Only a burdened heart can lead to fruitful service.—ALAN REDPATH

FRIENDSHIP

God evidently does not intend us all to be rich, or powerful, or great, but He does intend us all to be friends.—EMERSON

If you want to get rid of a friend, just tell him something for his own good.

To destroy your enemy, make him your friend.

A friend is one with whom you dare to be yourself.

A friend never gets in your way except when you are on the way down.

Friendship consists of forgetting what one gives and remembering what one receives.—ALEXANDER DUMAS

FORGIVENESS

In taking revenge a man is but equal to his enemy but in passing it over he is his superior.—BACON

A retentive memory may be a good thing but there is something to be said for the ability to forget.

FAILURE

Past failures become guideposts to future success.

FATHER

The most important thing a father can do for his children is to love their mother.

FORTUNE

Fortune does not change men. It only unmasks them.

FAULTFINDING

Nothing is easier than faultfinding; no talent, no self-denial, no brains, no character is required to set up in the grumbling business.

When I was young I resolved not to get married until I met the ideal woman. Some years later I found her—but she was looking for the ideal man.— MICHEL SIMON

Faultfinders never improve things; they just make things seem worse than it really is.

FLATTERY

Compliments are like perfume, to be inhaled but never swallowed.—C. C. MUNN

We would rather be ruined by praise than saved by criticism.

FELLOWSHIP

Like spokes in a wagon wheel, we find ourselves closer to each other as we draw closer to Christ the hub and center of life.

FRAGRANCE

Fragrance is like light. It cannot be hidden. It is like love: intangible, invisible, but always at once recognized. Though it is neither to be touched, nor heard, or seen, we know that it is there. And its opposite is just as impossible to hide. This brings us to a solemn truth: it is what we are that tells.— AMY CARMICHAEL

GREATNESS

There never was any heart truly great and gracious that was not also tender and compassionate.—SOUTH

God's giants have been weak men who did great things for God because they reckoned on His being with them.—HUDSON TAYLOR

Great men are those who see that the spiritual is stronger than any material force; that thoughts rule the world.—RALPH WALDO EMERSON

Men owe the grandeur of their lives to their many difficulties.—CHARLES SPURGEON

Big men become big by doing what they didn't want to do when they didn't want to do it.

The greatness of a man is measured by the length of the shadow he leaves as he recedes into history.

GOODNESS

The serene silent beauty of a holy life is the most powerful influence in the world, next to the might of God.—PASCAL

GRUDGE

An unfailing mark of a blockhead is the chip on his shoulder.

GENEROSITY

We make a living by what we get but we make a life by what we give.

When it comes to giving some people will stop at nothing.

What I spent I had; what I kept I lost; what I gave I
have.

GRANDMOTHER

Just about the time a woman thinks her work is done,
she becomes a grandmother.

GARDENING

A husband should not plant more than his wife can
hoe, weed and harvest.

In the garden you hoe, hoe, hoe, and if you think
that's funny you've never had a garden.

GREED

When a man dies he clutches in his hands only that
which he has given away in his lifetime.—
ROUSSEAU

GOD

God must first do something for us and in us, before
He can do something through us.

God gives Himself to us only in the measure in which
we give ourselves to Him.

When God is going to do something wonderful, He
begins with a difficulty; if He is going to do some-
thing very wonderful, He begins with an impossi-
bility.

God exempts no one from trouble but He will help us
through them.

The highways of history are strewn with the wreck-
age of nations that forgot God.

Calvary shows how far men will go in sin, and how far God will go for man's salvation.—H. C. TRUMBULL

Life's greatest tragedy is to lose God and never miss Him.

God is not a cosmic bell-boy for whom we can press a button to get things.—HARRY EMERSON FOSDICK

God is in the facts of history as truly as He is in the march of the seasons.—JOHN LANAHAN

God's ultimate purpose is unchanging, but his strategy may vary infinitely.—P. T. FORSYTH

Our Heavenly Father never takes anything from His children unless He means to give them something better.—GEORGE MUELLER

God is more interested in making us what He wants us to be than giving us what we ought to have.—WALTER WILSON

Contemporary religion has made God out to be a foolish grandfather, a bestower of spiritual sweet meats and celestial circus tickets.—BERNARD BELL

GUIDANCE

Two things will never happen to me—the thing that is too much for me, and the thing that is not best for me.—A. R. BROWN

GIVING

Some people don't let the left hand know what the right hand is giving because they don't want to embarass the right hand.

You give but little when you give of your possessions. It is when you give of yourself that you truly give. —KAHIL GIBRAN

You may give without loving but you cannot love without giving.

Fat pocket books are usually accompanied with a lean soul.

The Lord takes notice, not only of what we give, but also of what we have left.

GOSPEL

That the gospel is to be opposed is inevitable—disbelieved is to be expected—but that it should be made dull is intolerable—GERALD KENNEDY

When our clever sciences are forgotten, when all other stories pall, when the earth waxes old like a garment, the Gospel will still be young; it will still have power to untangle our raveled life; it will still win us to our hearts true home.—GEORGE BUT-TRICK

I have no fears that the candle lighted in Palestine years ago will ever be put out.—WILLIAM R. INGE

GOVERNMENT

Crooked politicians get into office because honest men fail to do their duty.

It is a poor economy to cut down on schools and later use the money on jails and reformatories.

No man is good enough to govern another without that other's consent.—ABRAHAM LINCOLN

GRIEF

Only the soul that knows the mighty grief can know the mighty rapture. Sorrow comes to stretch out spaces in the heart of joy.—EDWIN MARKHAM

Pleasures make folk acquainted with each other but it takes trials and griefs to make them know each other.—JOSH BILLINGS

GUIDANCE

I would rather walk with God in dark than go alone in the light.—MARY BRAINERD

GENERALIZATION

No generalization is wholly true, including this one. —DISRAELI

GENTLEMAN

A gentleman is always as nice as he sometimes is.

GOSSIP

People will believe anything if you whisper it.

GRATITUDE

When we were children we were grateful to those who filled our stockings with toys at Christmas time. Why are we not grateful to God for filling our stockings with legs.—G. K. CHESTERTON

There are two kinds of gratitude: the sudden kind we feel for what we take; the larger kind we feel for what we give.—EDWARD ARLINGTON ROBINSON

I would rather appreciate the things I do not have than to have the things I do not appreciate.—DORIAN TAYLOR

GOD'S WILL

Most people don't want to know the will of God in order to do it; they want to know it in order to consider it.—WILLIAM PETTINGILL

The will of God which we sometimes think so hard, is, if we only knew it, just the sofest pillow to rest upon.

What God calls a man to do, He will carry through. I would undertake to govern a half-million worlds if God called me to do it; but if He did not call me to do it, I would not undertake to govern half a dozen sheep.—PAYSON

It is great to do the Lord's work, but it is greater to do the Lord's will.—MIRIAM BOOTH

GLADNESS

You haven't fulfilled every duty until you have fulfilled the duty of being pleasant.—CHARLES BUXTON

HAPPINESS

There is no happiness in having and getting, but only in giving. Half the world is on the wrong scent in the pursuit of happiness.—F. W. GUNSAULUS

Unhappiness is the hunger to get. True happiness is the hunger to give.

Happiness is a perfume you cannot pour on others without getting a few drops on yourself.

Happiness is a hard thing because it is achieved only by making others happy.—STUART CLOETE

Think how happy you'd be if you lost everything you have right now—and then got it back again.— LEONARD M. LEONARD

One thing I know; the only ones among you who will be really happy are those who have sought and found how to serve.—ALBERT SCHWEITZER

When a happy man comes into a room it is as if another candle had been lit.—R. L. STEPHENSON

Success is getting what you want; happiness is wanting what you get.

Happiness is a thing to be daily practiced like a violin.

Happiness isn't so much a matter of position as it is of disposition.

Happiness is a butterfly, which when pursued is always just beyond your grasp, but which if you will sit down quietly will light upon you.—HAW-THORNE

Happiness comes when we sense we are of some use to somebody.

The quickest way to make yourself miserable is to start wondering whether you're as happy as you could be.

Never miss an opportunity to make someone happy, even if you have to let them alone to do it.

Happiness is that peculiar sensation one gets when he is too busy to be miserable.

After all it is not what is around us but what is in us; not what we have, but what we are, that makes us really happy.—GEIKE

The supreme happiness in life is the conviction of being loved for yourself or, more correctly, being loved in spite of yourself.

HELPFULNESS

Die when I may, I want it said of me by those who know me best, that I always plucked a thistle and planted a flower where I thought a flower would grow.—A. LINCOLN

There is no exercise better for the heart than reaching down and lifting people up.—JOHN HOLMER

There are two ways of exerting one's strength; one is pushing down, the other is pulling up.—BOOKER T. WASHINGTON

No man can sincerely try to help another without helping himself.—RALPH WALDO EMERSON

HOLY SPIRIT

He who has the Holy Spirit in his heart and the Scriptures in his hands has all he needs.—ALEXANDER MACLAREN

If there is not within us that which is above us, we shall soon yield to that which is around us.

HOPE

When hope is alive, the night is less dark, the solitude less deep, the fear less acute.

When it is dark enough men see the stars.—RALPH
WALDO EMERSON

There are no hopeless situations; there are only men
who have grown hopeless about them.—CLARE
BOOTHE LUCE

Even if I knew that tomorrow the world would go to
pieces, I would still plant my apple tree.—MARTIN
LUTHER

HUMILITY

In life we either learn humility or humiliation.

HYPOCRISY

Hypocrisy lies not in what you say to a person but
what you think of him.—FRANK ROONEY

HUSBAND

It is necessary to be almost a genius to make a good
husband.—BALZAC

When a wife has a good husband it is easily seen in
her face.—GOETHE

Getting a husband is like buying an old house. You
don't see it the way it is, but the way you think it's
going to be when you get it remodeled.

HUMOR

To go through life with no sense of the humorous and
ridiculous is like riding in an auto without springs
over a very rough road.

A good thing to have up your sleeve is a funny bone.

HOME

Home is where a fellow goes when he is tired of being nice to people.

HEAVEN

I am not tired of life but when the Lord calls me home I shall go with the gladness of a boy bounding away from school.—ADONIRAM JUDSON

In the Kingdom of the Spirit we belong to the place we are seeking for. In the charity of God we are as good as home when, though still a great way off, our faces are turned homeward.—HUTTON

HISTORY

He who will not learn from the lessons of history is condemned to live it over again.—GEORGE SANTYANA

The supreme purpose of history is a better world. Yesterday's records can keep us from repeating yesterday's mistakes.—HERBERT HOOVER

God is in facts of history as truly as he is in the march of the seasons.

HABIT

The chains of habit are generally too small to be felt until they are too strong to be broken.—SAMUEL JOHNSON

HEROISM

Life is meant to be a heroic thing. God's best gift to His greatest servants has not been immunity from suffering or death but heroic faith and uttermost trust.—GEORGE A. GORDEN

HEREDITY

Heredity is what makes the mother and father of teenagers wonder a little about each other.

HOUSEWORK

Housework is something you do that nobody notices unless you don't do it.

INHERITANCE

Could I climb to the highest place in Athens, I would lift my voice and proclaim—Fellow-citizens, why do you turn and scrape every stone to gather wealth, and take so little care of your children to whom one day you must relinquish it all.—SOCRATES

To reform a man you must begin with his grandmother.—VICTOR HUGO

America needs family trees that will produce more lumber and fewer nuts.

INJUSTICE

In the little world where children have their existence, there is nothing so finely perceived and so keenly felt as injustice.—CHARLES DICKENS

IMMORTALITY

Death is not a journeying into an unknown land; it is a voyage home. We are going not to a strange country but to our Father's house, and among our kith and kin.—JOHN RUSKIN

Death is not extinguishing the light; it is putting out the lamp because dawn has come.

But Hope sees a star, and in the night of death, listening love can hear the rustle of angel's wings.
—INGERSOLL

The best argument for an immortal life is the existence of a man who deserves it.—WILLIAM JAMES

If seeds in the black earth can turn into such beautiful flowers, what might the heart of man become in it's long journey toward the stars.

IDLENESS

The only thing necessary for the triumph of evil is for good men to do nothing.

Between the great things we cannot do and the little things we will not do, the danger is that we will do nothing.

Even if you are on the right track, you will get run over if you just sit there.

IMPOSSIBILITIES

Had Moses waited until he understood how Israel could elude Pharaoh's armies, they might have been in Egypt still.—MARTIN LUTHER

When you conclude a thing may not be achieved, look up and you'll probably see someone doing it.

The difficult we do at once. The impossible takes a little longer.—*Army Engineers motto*

INGRATITUDE

All our discomforts spring from the want of thankfulness for what we have.

A mild compliment timidly given in the spirit of restraint is an outrageous insult.

IMPROVEMENT

The church is not made up of people who are better than the rest, but of people who want to become better than they are.

The biggest room in the world is the room for improvement.

INFLUENCE

First I learned to love my teacher, then I learned to love my teacher's Bible, then I learned to love my teacher's Saviour.—MARION LAWRENCE

The serene silent beauty of a holy life is the most powerful influence in the world next to the might of the Spirit of God.—C. H. SPURGEON

INCARNATION

Since God came to earth as a baby and appeared in a manger, let us not be surprised to find Him anywhere.

INDECISION

Remember the uncertain soldier in the Civil War who figuring to play it safe, dressed himself in a blue coat and grey pants and tip-toed into the field of battle. He got shot from both directions.—PAUL HARVEY

INSPIRATION

Inspiration in presentation means perspiration in preparation.

IMPOSSIBILITY

Some people want to sit down and enjoy God all by themselves in a corner.—MARTIN LUTHER

INSTRUCTION

We learned long ago that we can prevent more crime in the high chair than in the electric chair.—J. EDGAR HOOVER

INTOXICATION

An intoxicated man is one who feels sophisticated but can't pronounce it.—VIC KNIGHT

When you try to drown your troubles in drink, you end up irrigating them.

He entered the bar fit as a fiddle. He left tight as a drum.

Intoxicants never enable a person to do his works better; it only makes him less ashamed to do them badly.—SIR WILLIAM OSLER

An alcoholic is just a social drinker who drinks between drinks.—WILLIAM RICHMER

INEQUITIES

A man's character is accurately measured by his reaction to life's inequities.

INCIDENTALS

Great happenings turn on hinges of little things.

INTEGRITY

It is better to follow the straight path than to move in the best circles.

INSIGHT

No affliction would trouble a child of God if he knew God's reasons for sending it—G. CAMPBELL MORGAN

IMPERFECTIONS

He who censures God, quarrels with the imperfections of men.—BURKE

IDEOLOGY

A Communist is one who borrows your pot to cook your goose in.

Communism says, "We will put a new suit of clothes on every man." Christ says, "I will put a new man in every suit of clothes."

INTOLERANCE

How a minority, reaching majority, seizing authority, hates a minority.—L. H. ROBBINS

INVESTMENT

Never invest your money in anything that eats or needs repainting.—BILLY ROSE

IDEALS

Words without action are the assassins of idealism. —HERBERT HOOVER

JUDGMENT

At the end of life God will not look us over for medals, diplomas, degrees or honors, but for scars.

God's judgment visits not only those who do evil but also those who fail to do good.

JESUS

The love of Jesus is both avid and generous. All that He is and all that He has, He gives. All that we are and all that we have, He takes.—VAN RUYS-BROECK

Jesus I think is the only soul in history who has truly appreciated the worth of man.—RALPH WALDO EMERSON

Is it any wonder that to this day this Galilean is too much for our small hearts.—H. G. WELLS

Again and again I have been tempted to give up the struggle but always the figure of that strange man hanging upon the cross sends me back to my task again.—MEISTER ECKHART

JOY

Sour godliness is the Devil's religion.—JOHN WESLEY

Real joy comes not from ease or riches or from the praise of men, but from doing something worthwhile.—SIR WILFRED GRENFELL

The devil would much rather put a long face on a Christian than to burn down the biggest church in town.

Joy is more divine than sorrow, for joy is bread and sorrow is medicine.—HENRY WARD BEECHER

Those who cannot feel pain are not capable of feeling joy either.—RADEN KARTINI

Grief can take care of itself but to get the full value of a joy you must have somebody to divide it with.—MARK TWAIN

JUDGING

You can judge a man pretty well by whether if given a choice, he asks for a lighter load or a stronger back.

JUSTICE

One hour in doing justice is worth a hundred hours in prayer.

Man's capacity for justice makes democracy possible, but man's inclination to injustice makes democracy necessary.—REINHOLD NIEBUHR

JUVENILES

Remember, it isn't the urge to deliberately do something bad that leads a boy or girl into crime. It's the urge to do something!—J. EDGAR HOOVER

Happy laughter and friendly voices in the home will keep more kids off the street at night than the loudest curfew.—BURTON HILLIS

KINGDOM

Above all things do not touch Christianity unless you are willing to seek the Kingdom of God first. I promise you a miserable existence if you seek it second.—HENRY DRUMMOND

If you do not wish God's kingdom, don't pray for it.
But if you do, you must do more than pray for it,
you must work for it.—RUSKIN

KINDNESS

You cannot do a kindness too soon because you never
know how soon it will be too late.

We're often remorseful for speaking harshly but
have you ever known one regretful for speaking
kindly?

Colors fade, temples crumble, empires fall, seasons
change, but kind words endure forever.

Kindness has converted more sinners than either zeal,
eloquence or learning.—F. W. FABER

One can pay back a loan of gold, but one dies forever
in debt to those who are kind.

Kindness is the truest revealer of a person's great-
ness.

Most bread cast upon the water returns with butter
and jam on it.

The older you get the more you realize that kindness
is synonymous with happiness.—LIONEL BARRY-
MORE

The secret of success in conversation is to be able to
disagree without being disagreeable.

A part of kindness consists in loving people more
than they deserve.—JOSEPH JOUBERT

KNOWLEDGE

A good listener is not only popular everywhere but after a while he knows something.

Knowledge and intelligence, like a river, make less noise as it gets deeper.

After all, the two most important things to learn are, where to find the knowledge you need, and how to get along without it.

LOYALTY

If absence makes the heart grow fonder, think how much some people must love the church.

LABOR

Nothing is as ·fatal to character as a half-finished task.—David Lloyd George

Little do you know your own blessedness; for to travel hopefully is a better thing than to arrive, and the true success is to labor.—R. L. Stephenson

To love life through labor is to be intimate with life's inmost secret.

It is almost as presumptuous to think you can do nothing as to think you can do everything.—Phillips Brooks

Small worries are like gnats; movement and activity disperse them.—Gustav

LIFE

We must make up for the threatened brevity of life by heightening the intensity of life.—Joshua Liebman

We are not here to doubt or hesitate about things, but to live our lives once for all with all our strength. —JOHN HUTTON

To live without working is as wrong as to work without living.

The great use of life is to spend it for something that outlasts it.

Life can only be understood backward, but it must be lived forward.—KIERKEGAARD

Life is a grindstone: whether it grinds you down or polishes you up depends on what you're made of.

To be a Christian in a real sense is far more than wearing a label. It means living a life.

It is impossible to cheat life. There are no answers to the problems of life in the back of the book.— KIERKEGAARD

LIVING

Jesus never taught men how to make a living. He taught men how to live.—BOB JONES, SR.

To live well in the quiet routine of life, to fill a little space because God wills it, to go on cheerfully with a petty routine of little duties; to smile for the joy of others when the heart is aching—who does this, his works will follow him. He may not be a hero to the world, but he is one of God's heroes.

LOVE

The way to love anything is to realize that it may be lost.—G. K. CHESTERTON

Someday, after mastering the winds, the waves, the tides, and gravity, we shall harness for God the energies of love, and then, for the second time in the history of the world, man will discover fire. —TEILHARD DE CHARDIN

Riches take wings, comforts vanish, hope withers away, but love stays with us. God is love.—LEW WALLACE

Love is the irresistible desire to be irresistibly desired.—ROBERT FROST

It took me a long time to learn that God is not the enemy of my enemies. He is not even the enemy of His enemies.—MARTIN NIEMOELLER

We love those we are happy with. We do! For how else can we know we love them or how else define loving.—NAN FAIRBROTHER

Love at first sight is possible but it's a wise man who takes a good second look.

Love is a strange bewilderment which overtakes one person on account of another person.—JAMES THURBER

Love doesn't consist in gazing at each other but in looking outward together in the same direction.

LAUGHTER

Laughter is the sensation of feeling good all over and showing it principally in one spot.—JOSH BILLINGS

I am persuaded that every time a man smiles, but much more when he laughs, it adds something to this fragment of life.—STERNE

LAZINESS

If the ships of some men did come in, they would be too lazy to unload them.

Our church is composed of such willing people. Some are willing to work and others are willing to let them.

LONELINESS

How foolish we are to spend our lives building walls around our private estates, and then complain how lonely we are.

LONGING

There is not a heart but has its moments of longing, yearning for something better, nobler, holier than it knows now.—HENRY WARD BEECHER

LEADERSHIP

You can accomplish almost anything if you don't care who gets the credit.

A free people can be led a greater distance and to greater heights than a slave can be driven.—DAVID SARNOFF

LEADERS

The little sins of great men are often responsible for the great sins of little men.—JOHN TIMOTHY STONE

LIBERAL

Some liberal churches let their ministers preach on any topic except politics and religion.

LISTENING

Some talkative people do not grasp why they were given two ears and only one tongue.

LUCK

I am a great believer in luck. The harder I work, the more luck I seem to have.—EMERSON

LEISURE

What we are comes to light when we are free to do what we like.

LIGHT

There are two ways of spreading light: to be the candle or the mirror that reflects it.—EDITH WHARTON

LONGEVITY

Everybody wants to live longer but nobody wants to grow old.

God allows us just enough time for the work which He allots us.

LIBERTY

God grants liberty only to those who love it, and are always ready to guard and defend it.—DANIEL WEBSTER

MISSION

If you want to follow Christ you must follow Him to the ends of the earth for that is where He is going.
—ROBERT E. SPEER

79

There's no better exercise for strengthening the heart than reaching down and lifting up people.

You can never speak to the wrong man about Christ.
—MacFarlane

I am afraid we sometimes pray that God may help us to accomplish some great and mighty task when we ought rather to pray that He may teach us how to give a cup of cold water in Jesus's name.—C. H. Touchberry, Sr.

A vision without work is visionary; work without a vision is mercenary; together they mean missionary.

The missionary can know that he has been sent, that he is safe and that he is supplied by God.—Alan Redpath

MONUMENT

The monument I want after I am dead is a monument with two legs going around the world—a saved sinner talking about the salvation of Jesus Christ.
—Dwight L. Moody

MOTIVES

We always judge ourselves by our motives. Why then judge others by their actions?

MISQUOTE

The Lord is my shepherd, I can do what I want.

MONEY

Money may not be the measure of a man but it does reveal how small he is.

It's better to have your bank in heaven than to have your heaven in a bank.

Money speaks but it's owner is it's only interpreter.

Money is an article which may be used as a universal passport to everywhere except Heaven, and as a universal provider of everything except happiness.

It is good to have money and the things that money can buy, but it is good to check up once in a while and make sure you haven't lost the things money can't buy.—GEORGE LORIMER

It's not a sin to be rich, it's a miracle.

Some say you can hardly go to heaven and be rich, but I for one would love to try.

Every man goes down to his grave clutching in his cold hands only that which he has given away.

Money isn't everything but it is way ahead of second best.

Money doesn't necessarily make one happy but it helps one enjoy his misery.

MANKIND

I believe that man will not merely endure; he will prevail. He is immortal, not because he alone among creatures has an inexhaustible voice, but because he has a soul, a spirit capable of compassion and sacrifice and endurance.—WILLIAM FAULKNER

A million years from now earth may be filled with creatures who stoutly deny that they ever descended from man.

People wouldn't get divorced for such trivial reasons if they didn't get married for such trivial reasons. —BOB GANARD

It has almost reached the point where marriage is sufficient ground for divorce.

Lots of girls would make better wives if they weren't foolishly trying to make better husbands.

Marriage is more than finding the right person. It is being the right person.

A wife laughs at her husband's jokes not because they are clever but because she is.

The difference between a good marriage and a bad one is leaving a few words unsaid each day.

Very few men realize how short they fall of perfection until they possess a wife. —JOAN KENNEDY

A successful marriage requires falling in love many times, always with the same person. —MIGNON MCLAUGHLIN

Marriage is like the army: everybody complains but you'd be surprised how many re-enlist.

Why does a woman work ten years to change a man's habits and then complain that he's not the man she married. —BARBARA STRIESAND

Marriage is like a violin—after the music is over the strings are still attached.

In Genesis it says that it is not good for a man to be alone—but sometimes it is a great relief. —JOHN BARRYMORE

Marriages may be made in heaven but they still have to be lived on earth.

Grecian ladies counted their age from their marriage, not from their birth.—HOMER

Keep your eyes wide open before marriage and half shut afterwards.—BENJAMIN FRANKLIN

A honeymoon is the period between "I do" and "You'd better!"

The secret of successful marriage is to treat disasters as incidents and to never treat incidents as disasters.

Marriage is one game where two can play and both lose.

When one man loves one woman and one woman loves one man, the very angels desert heaven and come and sit in that house and sing for joy.

It's not marriage that fails; it is the people that fail. All that marriage does is show people up.

It is not lack of love but lack of friendship that makes unhappy marriages.

A happy marriage is a long conversation that always seems too short.—MAUROIS

When a girl marries she exchanges the attentions of many men for the inattention of one.—HELEN ROWLAND

Fewer marriages would end in court if more time were spent in courting.

Some women work so hard to make good husbands that they never quite manage to make good wives.

Often the difference between a successful marriage and a mediocre one consists of leaving about three or four things a day unsaid.

Most newlyweds possess special talent for seeing each other's faults.

All that a husband or wife really wants is to be pitied a little, praised a little, appreciated a little and for each to realize that the hard work is not all on one side.—WARREN GOLDSMITH

Wounded vanity is fatal to love. It makes one hate the person who inflicted the wound. In married conversation, as in surgery, the knife must be used with care.—MAUROIS

Marriage is a process of finding out what sort of guy your wife would have preferred.—STRICKLAND GILLILAN

They're married for better or worse. He couldn't do better and she couldn't do worse.

MOTTO

Live without worry, work without hurry, and advance without fear.

MEMORY

If you can make children happy now, you will make them happy twenty years hence by the memory of it.—KATE WIGGIN

God has given us memory that we might have roses in December.—JAMES BARRIE

MOTHERS

Somewhere it must be written that the virtues of the mothers shall be visited on their children as well as the sins of the fathers.—CHARLES DICKENS

Mother is the name of God in the lips and hearts of little children.—WILLIAM M. THACKERY

A mother is not a person to lean on but a person to make leaning unnecessary.—DOROTHY FISHER

To a man who has had a Christian mother, all women are sacred for her sake.—JEAN PAUL RICHTER

MAN

We have learned to fly through the air like birds and to swim through the sea like fish. When will we learn to walk the earth like men?

Usually the self-made man who worships his creator, knocked off too soon.

A gentleman is always as nice as he sometimes is.

NEGLECT

Most of today's troubles on which we stub our toes are the unpleasant, unperformed duties that we carelessly shoved aside yesterday.

NATURE

The landscape belongs to the man who looks at it.—RALPH WALDO EMERSON

If God had been here last summer and had seen some
things I saw, I am sure He would have thought
His upper heaven superflous.—EMILY DICKEN-
SON

Nature is wonderful! A million years ago she didn't
know we were going to wear spectacles, yet look at
the way she placed our ears.

If spring came once in a century instead of once a
year or burst forth with the sound of an earth-
quake, and not in silence, what wonder and expec-
tation there would be in all hearts to behold the
miraculous change.—HENRY W. LONGFELLOW

NEW BIRTH

No man is high born until he is born from on high.

NEW YEAR

May all our troubles during the coming year be as
short-lived as our New Year's resolutions.—BETTY
RAMSEY

NOBILITY

The best manner of avenging ourselves is by not
resembling him who has injured us.—JANE POR-
TER

NATION

We cannot live the way we have been living without
having the kind of world we now have.—E.
STANLEY JONES

Some men live to be fifty or sixty before they have a chance. I had my chance at nineteen and took it.—Final words of WILLIAM MCLAUGHLIN, hero of the Iroquois Theater fire in Chicago

Don't waste time looking for four leaf clovers when there are weeds in your garden.

When God shuts a door, He always opens a window.

The surest way to go broke is to sit around waiting for a break.

To kill time is to murder opportunity.

If opportunity knocked on some people's heads instead of their doors, she'd get better results.

Opportunity doesn't knock at the door—she answers when you knock.—WALTER L. HAYS

If fate throws a knife at you there are two ways of catching it—by the blade or by the handle.

It is one of the hardships of life that when one has sufficient knowledge to enjoy a particular sort of existence, the opportunity has invaribly passed.—A. K. QUILTER

OBEDIENCE

One of the first things a man notices in a backward nation is that children there are still obeying their parents.—CLAUDE CALLAN

Rather than violate the known will of God, I would forfeit my life.—STONEWALL JACKSON

A child has to learn obedience in the home or he will never learn obedience to the Heavenly Father.

OBSTACLES

Obstacles are those frightful things you see when you take your eyes off the goal.

OPPOSITION

Most of us carry our own stumbling block around with us; we camouflage it with a hat.—MARK ALKUS

The door to the room of success swings on the hinges of opposition.

OPPORTUNIST

An opportunist is a man who, finding himself in hot water, decides he needs a bath anyway.

An opportunist is a woman who finds the wolf at the door and later appears in a fur coat.

ORTHODOXY

You may be as orthodox as the Devil, and as wicked. —JOHN WESLEY

OPTIMISM

The optimist is as often wrong as the pessimist, but he is far happier.

Some people are always grumbling because roses have thorns. I am thankful that thorns have roses. —ALPHONSE KARR

You'll never get eye strain from looking on the bright side of things.

The pessimist sees difficulties in every opportunity. The optimist sees opportunity in every difficulty.

When an optimist gets the worst of it, he makes the best of it.

Either make light of your woes, or keep them in the dark.

OPINIONS

A string of opinions no more constitutes faith than a string of beads constitutes holiness—JOHN WESLEY

OLD AGE

When one gets too old to set a bad example he starts giving good advice.

OVERCOMING

When any calamity has been suffered, the first thing to be remembered is how much has been escaped. —SAMUEL JOHNSON

OUTLOOK

Religion is not a way of looking at certain things, but a certain way of looking at all things.

ORIGINALITY

When everyone agrees, there is very little thinking.

PEACE

The peace of God passes all understanding and mis-understanding.

We're paying installments on wars we aren't using anymore while saving up for a war we do not want.

PREACHING

Jesus, the good shepherd, did not say, "Club my sheep." He said, "Feed my sheep."

Use what language you will, you can never say anything but what you are.

The essence of the minister lies in what God has created him to be rather than in what the church authorized him to do.—JOHN STACEY

The greatest gift that ever comes from the minister to his people is the gift of getting them to understand and pursue the way of prayer.—JAMES A. JONES

Only once did God choose a completely sinless preacher.—ALEXANDER WHYTE

If you make people think they're thinking, they'll love you; but if you really make them think, they'll hate you.—DON MARQUIS

To say what you mean without ever offending people is usually to say what you mean without making them believe you mean what you say.—JAMES HILTON

Fill the people and the people will fill the pews.

He who has truth in his heart need never fear the want of persuasion on his tongue.

It is not enough that there should be action in the pulpit—there must be reaction in the pews.—CALVIN COOLIDGE

PATIENCE

Is it not heartening to see some pilgrim who is broken in body but who retains the unbroken splendor of an unbroken patience?—J. H. JOWETT

It is not miserable to be blind. It is miserable to be incapable of enduring blindness.

POWER

And so when God wants to bring more power into your life, he brings more pressure.—A. B. SIMPSON

The task ahead of us is never as great as the Power behind us.

The descent of the Holy Spirit was preceded, precipitated, and perpetuated by prayer.

PURPOSE

It is not the will of God to give us more troubles than will bring us to live by truth in Him; He loves us too well to give us a moment of uneasiness unless it is for our good.—JULES ROMAINS

We can always live on less when we have more to live for.

If God is your partner, make your plans big.

The only man worth envying is the one who has found a cause bigger than himself.—GUY WRIGHT

God never wasted a leaf on a tree; do you think he would squander souls?—RUDYARD KIPLING

I find the great thing in this world is not so much
where we stand, as in what direction we are
moving.—OLIVER WENDELL HOLMES

PRAYER

Prayer is a silent surrender of everything to God.—
SOREN KIERKEGAARD

When I pray coincidences happen and when I do not,
they don't.—WILLIAM TEMPLE

To speak for God to men is a sacred and responsible
task. To speak for men to God is not less responsi-
ble and is more solemn.—ROBERT DABNEY

Prayer may begin by asking God for what we want.
It will end more interested in what He wants.

Who rises from prayer a better man, his prayer is
answered.—MEREDITH

A family altar leads to an altered life.

To grow tall spiritually a man must learn to kneel.

Keep account of your prayers so you won't unsay
them in your deeds and practice.

He stands best who kneels most.

Prayer is the most important thing in my life. If I
should neglect prayer for a single day, I should
lose a great deal of the fire of faith.—MARTIN
LUTHER

The secret of prayer is prayer in secret.

Groanings which cannot be uttered are often prayers
which cannot be refused.—C. H. SPURGEON

No praying man or woman accomplishes so much with so little expenditure of time as when he or she is praying.—C. E. Cowman

I have so much to do that I must spend several hours in prayer before I am able to do it.—John Wesley

Prayerless pews make powerless pulpits.

PRACTICING

People may forget how fast you did a job, but they will never forget how well you did it.

Statistics prove that Americans spend more money on gum than they do on religion. They use gum every day.—Josephus Henry

PROSPERITY

A man is never so on trial as in the moment of excessive good fortune.—Lew Wallace

It takes a strong constitution to withstand repeated attacks of prosperity.

PROGRESS

You can't do today's job with yesterday's tools and be in business tomorrow.—Helen Mackintosh

We, unlike oarsmen, seldom go forward by looking backward.

PRESENT

Our main business is not to see what lies dimly at a distance but to do what lies clearly at hand.

PERSONALITY

Make other people like themselves a little better, my son, and I promise you they will like you very well.
—LORD CHESTERFIELD

PUNCTUALITY

The trouble with being punctual is that there is nobody there to appreciate it.

POVERTY

Poverty is uncomfortable, as I can testify; but nine times out of ten the best thing that can happen to a young man is to be tossed overboard and compelled to sink or swim for himself.—JAMES A. GARFIELD

Poverty is a virtue greatly overrated by those who no longer practice it.—BARNABY KEENEY

PERSECUTION

Stones and sticks are thrown only at fruit-bearing trees.—SAADI

PRAISE

The deepest principle of human nature is the craving to be appreciated.—WILLIAM JAMES

PARENTS

It's better to be a good gardener than a poor parent; you can throw out spoiled vegetables, but spoiled children you have to keep.—MUNDAY SMITH

In most modern homes everything is run by switches except the kids.

The great, the astonishing thing about youth is that it may be enjoyed twice! Once through one's own youth and later and better through that of another. —PHILLIP BARRY

When we are out of sympathy with the young, then I think our work in this world is over.—MAC DONALD

Children begin by loving their parents; as they grow older they judge them; sometimes they forgive them.—OSCAR WILDE

The cure of crime is not the electric chair, but the high chair.—J. EDGAR HOOVER

Call that man happy who, whatever ills he suffers, has a child to love.—ROBERT SOUTHY

If you must hold yourself up to your children as an object lesson, hold yourself up as a warning and not as an example.

The best safeguard for the younger generation is a good example by the older generation.

PERFECTION

Only those who have the patience to do simple things perfectly, ever acquire the skill to do difficult things easily.—SCHILLER

PRIDE

The bigger a man's head gets, the easier is it to fill his shoes.

PROTEST

To sin by silence when they should protest makes cowards of men.

PERSISTENCE

Our greatest glory is not in never failing but in rising every time we fall.—CONFUCIUS

QUIETNESS

Well-timed silence is more eloquent than speech.— MARTIN TUPPER

I have oft regretted my speech—never my silence.— PUBLIUS SYRUS

Be silent and safe! Has silence ever betrayed you?

A quiet spirit is of inestimable value in carrying on outward activities.—HANNAH W. SMITH

Quiet minds cannot be perplexed or frightened, but go on in fortune or misfortune at their own private pace, like a clock during a thunderstorm.—ROBERT LOUIS STEVENSON

QUITTING

The Christian life is like an airplane; when you stop, you drop.

The greatest calamity is not to have failed but to have failed to try again.

QUARRELLING

To interfere with the quarrels of relatives is to go through life without a friend.

A quarrel is ended when one refuses.

READING

Show me a family of readers and I will show you the people who move the world.

Those who can read and don't read are no better off than those who can't read.

RETALIATION

How can you hope to get ahead of someone as long as you are trying to get even with him.

REFORM

Too many people get excited over plans for changing the world, but won't move a finger to improve conditions in their own home towns.—ERIC JOHNSTON

The best reformers are those who commence on themselves.

All reforms start at the bottom. Nobody ever heard of a man with four aces calling for a new deal.

RECREATION

People who don't play are potentially dangerous. There seems to be a general idea that recreation is all right if one doesn't take it too seriously. My belief is that the greater danger lies in not taking it seriously enough.—KARL MENNINGER

RESURRECTION

Our Lord has written the promise of the resurrection not in books alone, but in every leaf in springtime. —MARTIN LUTHER

The evidences for the resurrection are as strong as for the events on the fourth of July, 1776.—ROBERT E. SPEER

A man could retire wealthy if he could sell his experiences for what they cost him.

Without sufficient money, retirement becomes tragedy. Without good health it becomes misery. But even with sufficient wealth and good health, you will not be happy until you have something meaningful to do.—HARRY JOHNSON

RELIGION

It is a great mistake to suppose that God is only or even chiefly, concerned with religion.—WILLIAM TEMPLE

True religion is betting one's life that there is a God.
—DONALD HANKEY

What I want is not to possess religion, but to have a religion that possesses me.—CHARLES KINGSLEY

If we make religion our business, God will make it our blessedness.—H. G. J. ADAMS

Religion is what the individual does with his own solitude; if you are never solitary, you are never religious.

Religion is the life of God in the soul of man.—LYMAN ABBOT

No religion is irrelevant if it helps people to see the hidden glory of the common things they do.—ELTON TRUEBLOOD

Too many people regard religion as a trolly car on which they ride only as long as it is going their way.

Religion is not a way of looking at certain things, but a certain way of looking at all things.

Some want a religion that makes them feel respectable without requiring them to be.

People are not interested in religion but in reality.—HENRIETTA MEARS

The religion that makes a man look sick certainly won't cure the world.

More than a definition of religion, we need a demonstration.

Poor religion is strong only when the owner is in trouble.

Dead is the religion which does not aim at these two things: personal purity and active charity.—THOMAS GUTHRIE

The trouble with us is that we have been inoculated with small does of Christianity which keep us from catching the real thing.—LESLIE WEATHERHEAD

A certain churchmember was like a farmer's well; it froze up in winter and dried up in summer.

Religion's business is to make business religious.

Among all my patients in the second half of life, that is to say, past thirty-five, there has not been one whose problem in the last resort has not been that of finding a religious outlook on life.—KARL MENNINGER

Religion, like music, is not in need of defense, but rendition.—HARRY EMERSON FOSDICK

REJECTION

If Jesus Christ were to come today, people would not crucify Him. They would ask him to dinner and hear what he had to say—and make fun of it.—D. A. WILSON

RETRIBUTION

If you walk to the edge of a cliff and keep on going straight ahead, you will not break the law of gravity, you will prove it.—G. K. CHESTERTON

REPUTATION

A man's reputation is what his friends say about him. His character is what his enemies say about him.

REPENTANCE

You cannot repent too soon because you know not how soon it may be too late.

He who finds it easy to repent will find it easy to sin.
—F. E. HULME

REWARD

The world's most disappointed people are those who get what's coming to them.

REVENGE

The noblest revenge is to forgive.—THOMAS FULLER

SPEECH

The jawbone of an ass was a killer in Samson's time. It still is.—MORRIS GILBERT

Some people are not merely dogmatic but bull dogmatic.

100

Little people talk about people. Average people talk about happenings. Great people talk about ideas.

Take a lesson from the whale: the only time he gets harpooned is when he comes up to spout.

Blessed is the man, who, having nothing to say, abstains from giving wordy evidence of it.

Talk to God about your neighbors, and talk to your neighbors about God.

There is nothing wrong in having nothing to say unless you insist on saying it.

One reason why a dog is such a lovable creature is that his tail wags instead of his tongue.

Remember not only to say the right thing in the right place, but far more difficult still, to leave unsaid the wrong thing at the tempting moment.— BENJAMIN FRANKLIN

Two things indicate weakness—to be silent when it is proper to speak and to speak when it is proper to be silent.

Ninety per cent of the friction of daily life is caused by the tone of voice.—ARNOLD BENNETT

A fish could stay out of trouble if it could keep its mouth closed.

There are times when it is better to keep your mouth shut at the risk of being considered an ignoramus, than to open it and remove all doubt about it.— J. E. HEDGES

If one remains silent long enough, observers begin to think of him as a philosopher.

It's better to keep your mouth shut and be thought a fool than it is to open it and prove it.

To be a good speaker stand up to be seen, speak up to be heard, and sit down to be appreciated.

Is there any significance to the fact that when a woman says she's all tired out, the doctor first looks at her tongue?—MAYNERD BRADFORD

No spoken indiscretion was ever so bitterly regretted as the words one did not speak.—JAN STRUTHER

The art of saying appropriate words in a kindly way is one that never goes out of fashion, never ceases to please and is within the reach of the humblest.
—F. W. FABER

It often shows a fine command of language to say nothing.

SELF-HELP

The best place to find a helping hand is at the end of your arm.—EARL WILSON

SIN

Sin is the only thing in the universe of which it may be truly said, "The more you practice it, the less you know of its nature."—MARTINEAU

It is not enough for the gardener to love flowers; he must also hate weeds.

SHARING

Don't share your troubles; people are already over supplied.

You cannot kindle a fire in any other heart until it is burning within your own.

SUCCESS

Behind every successful man there is a woman—constantly reminding him he's not so hot.

Some men think they have made a success of life when all they have made is money.

No man is a failure who is enjoying life.

Success consists of getting up just one more time than you fall.

There are three types of people: those who make things happen, those who watch things happen, and the vast majority who have no idea what happens.

A man may fail many times, but he isn't a failure until he begins to blame someone else.

It is more important to make something of ourselves than for ourselves.

SURRENDER

I will place no value on anything I have or may possess except in relation to the Kingdom of Christ.—DAVID LIVINGSTONE

We either let God go or else let go and let God.

SITUATION

I'm up a tree with my back against the wall and my nose to the grindstone. Yet I'll paddle my own canoe and fight to the last ditch regardless of the enemy that barks at my heels. May I go down hurling defiance at the foe and with my flag flying, soaring on wings of triumph and standing steadfast at my post of duty.

SALVATION

Some people plan to be saved at the eleventh hour but die at ten-thirty.

While salvation is free, it is not cheap.

SICKNESS

It is a poor religion that is never strong except when the owner is sick.

SERMON

A good sermon consists in saying all that is necessary and nothing that is unnecessary.

Sermonettes are fine for Christianettes.

SEPARATION

A ship is safe in the ocean as long as the ocean is not in the ship, and a Christian is safe in the world so long as the world is not in the Christian.

STRENGTH

Instead of praying for an easier task, pray to grow stronger.

SELF-RIGHTEOUSNESS

It's easier to sail the Atlantic in a paper boat than to get to heaven on good works.

SHEEP

Some people count sheep and some people talk to the Shepherd.

STUDY

We must apply ourselves wholly to the scriptures and the scriptures wholly to us.

SECRET

How can we expect our friends to keep a secret when we are unable to conceal it ourselves?

SPORTS

I have never felt that football built character. This is done by parents and church. You give us a boy with character and we will give you back a man. You give us a boy of character and we will give him right back to you.—JOHN McKAY

SELF-CONTROL

Never expect to govern others until you have learned to govern yourself.

SELF-CENTEREDNESS

The smallest of all packages is the person wrapped up in himself, and usually he is fit to be tied.

SERVICE

Once the will of God to me was a sigh; now it is a song.—FRANCES R. HAVERGAL

One can be serious without being sour.

Instead of waiting on the Lord, some people want the Lord to wait on them.

Selfishness is the great unknown sin. No selfish person ever thought himself selfish.

Hardening of the heart ages people more quickly than hardening of the arteries.

God gets his best soldiers out of the highlands of affliction.

If God sends us on strong paths He will provide us with strong shoes.—ALEXANDER MACLAREN

Troubles that you borrow soon become your own.

Storms make oaks to send down deeper roots.

I have lived a long life and I have known lots of trouble but most of it never happened.

Life is easy! All you have to do is accept the impossible, do without the indispensable, and bear the intolerable.

Blessed to us is the night, for it reveals the stars to us.

If life gives you a lemon just squeeze it and make a lemonade.

Nobody knows the trouble we see, but we keep trying to tell people.

God will not permit any troubles to come upon us, unless He has a specific plan by which great blessing can come out of the difficulty.—PETER MARSHALL

TRUTH

Now whatever be the truth that the mind seeks, it can only move towards truth along one road, and on that road there are three stages. The first is WONDER, the second is VISION, the third is VENTURE. There is no other road to the palace of TRUTH.—CLOW

Truth must not be manipulated. It is better to wash one's dirty linen in public than to wear it in public. —PHILIP SCHARPER

Time, whose teeth gnaw away everything else, is powerless against truth.

To poison a man's mind is a worse sin than to poison his food.

TIME

The years teach much which the days never knew.— RALPH WALDO EMERSON

Yesterday is a cancelled check; tomorrow is a promissory note; today is ready cash, spend it.

The times in which we live are decadent. It is evident we are approaching the end of the age. Everyone has disregarded the law. Children no longer obey their parents. Everyone is eager to write a book.— *Inscribed on Chaldean tablet 2000* B.C.

TACT

Tact is the knack of making a point without making an enemy.—HOWARD NEWTON

A compromise is the art of dividing a cake in such a way that everyone believes he has received the biggest piece.—LUDWIG ERHARD

Tact is the unsaid part of what you think.

Tact is the ability to extract the stinger without getting stung.

Tact is the ability to close your mouth before someone else wants to.

TOLERANCE

Tolerance is the bigness that enables us to want those we love to be happy in their own way instead of ours.

TALKING

It takes two years for a baby to learn to talk and the rest of life to learn to keep his mouth shut.

To save face, keep the lower part closed.

THINKING

We need not all think alike but we should all think.

Some minds are like concrete: all mixed up and permanently set.

TIPPING

Tipping has been defined as paying wages to other people's hired help.

If you can't be thankful for what you receive, be thankful for what you escape.

I would rather appreciate the things I do not have than to have the things I do not appreciate.— DORIAN TAYLOR

TEMPER

Men are like steel—when they lose their temper they are worthless.

The measure of a man is the things it takes to get his goat.

TRUST

All I have seen teaches me to trust the Creator for what I have not seen.—RALPH WALDO EMERSON

Trust marches at the head of the army of progress. It is found beside the most refined life, the freest government, the profoundest philosophy, the noblest poetry, the purest humanity.—T. T. MONGER

In actual life every great enterprise begins with and takes its first forward step in faith.—SCHLEGAL

There is something better than understanding God; that is trusting him.—G. H. KNIGHT

TRIALS

Great trials seem to be necessary preparation for great duties.

TEARS

God washes the eyes with tears until they can behold the invisible land where tears shall come no more.

TESTIMONY

If a person is a socialist or Communist I will know it in twenty-four hours; if he is a member of a labor union I will know it within a few days; but if he is a member of the Christian church it may be years before I will ever learn of it.—WAGNER

THINKING

As people should not eat if they don't work, so people should not talk if they don't think.

TEMPTATION

No man knows how bad he is until he has tried very hard to be good. There is a silly idea going that good people don't know what temptation means.—C. S. LEWIS

Temptations are like tramps. Treat them kindly and they return bringing others with them.

TRANQUILITY

I keep the telephone of my mind open to peace, harmony, health, love and abundance. Then whenever doubt, anxiety or fear try to call me, they keep getting the busy signal—and they'll soon forget my number.—EDITH ARMSTRONG

TALENT

Use what talents you possess: the woods would be very silent if no birds sang except those that sang best.—HENRY VAN DYKE

TEACHER

A teacher is late unless he is a half-hour early.

He who teaches the Bible is never a scholar; he is always a student.

The art of teaching is not imparting truth but imparting a thirst for truth.

What you say and how you say it is important but how you live is most important.

The teacher is the hinge on which the Sunday School swings.

Good teachers cost much but poor teachers cost more.

Children brought up in Sunday School are seldom brought up in court.

The longer I teach the more I am impressed with the infinite capacity of the human mind to resist the introduction of knowledge.—LOUNSBURY

THOUGHTFULNESS

Never part without loving words to think of during your absence. It may be that you will not meet again in life.—JEAN PAUL RICHTER

UNDERSTANDING

To understand is to forgive. Perhaps we might go a step farther and say to understand is to accept, sometimes even to love.—ELEANOR ROOSEVELT

The most important trip a man can make is that involved in meeting the other fellow half way.—BRICE VAN HORN

Everywhere husbands and wives have at least one thing in common, to see each others faults.

There would be less fear in the world if there were more understanding.

How lucky we are that people don't fully understand us. They couldn't stand it.

Believe me, every man has his secret sorrows, which the world knows not; and oftentimes we call a man cold when he is only sad.—HENRY WADSWORTH LONGFELLOW

If we could read the secret history of our enemies, we would find in each man's life sorrow and suffering enough to disarm all hostility.—LONGFELLOW

If misunderstood, don't worry. If you can't understand, start worrying.

There are two times when a man doesn't understand a woman—before marriage and after.

I do not agree with a word you say but I will defend to death your right to say it.—VOLTAIRE

UNITY

United notions may be more important now than United Nations.

UPBRINGING

Let every father and mother realize that when their child is three years of age, they have done more than half they will ever do for its character.—HORACE BUSHNELL

UNKINDNESS

Hardening of the heart ages more people more quickly than hardening of the arteries.— FRANKLIN FIELD

VACATION

Religion is not a fur coat to be put away in moth balls during the summer months.

The thrill of getting back home is the most enjoyable feature of a summer vacation.

A vacation is recreation preceded by anticipation and followed by recuperation.

VISION

Other people can't make you see with their eyes. They can only encourage you to use your own.

A teacher or a preacher without a great vision will end up dreaming troubled dreams.

VOCATION

The business of the Christian is to give direction to change.

The vocation of every man and woman is to serve other people.—LEO TOLSTOY

VALUES

When mentioning things you can't afford, remember to include pride, envy, and malice.

Without bread a man does not live long. If bread is all he gets he cannot live well.—R. F. AUMAN

Some things can't be measured; we do not think of a ton of truth, a bushel of beauty, or an inspiration a mile long.—JOSEPH FORT NEWTON

Fools sacrifice things money can't buy or bring back, in order to obtain money.—G. JORDAN

When a man is born people say, "How is the Mother?" When he marries they say, "What a beautiful bride!" When he dies they say, "How much did he leave her?"

VIRTUE

Virtue consists, not in abstaining from vice, but in not desiring it.—GEORGE BERNARD SHAW

VICE

To be softened and weakened by vice is worse than being hardened and calloused by respectability.— SYDNEY HARRIS

VISION

A task without a vision is drudgery; a vision without a task is a dream; a task with a vision is victory.

Living on a mountain means having a longer day than those living in the valley. To have a brighter, longer life, climb higher.

The further backward you can look, the further forward you are likely to see.—WINSTON CHURCHHILL

WEALTH

A man is rich or poor according to what he is, not according to what he has.

The measure of a man's wealth is how much he would be worth if he lost his money.

Wealth is not only what you have but what you are. —STERLING SILL

He who teaches his child to be thrifty and economical has already bequeathed him a fortune. —RUTH SMELTZER

WITNESSING

You can never speak to the wrong man about Christ. —PETER McFARLANE

God hasn't retained many of us as lawyers, but he has subpoenaed all of us as witnesses.

If you want your neighbor to know what God can do for him, let him see what God has done for you.— HENRY WARD BEECHER

There is not enough darkness in the whole world to put out the light of a single candle.

A candle loses nothing by lighting another candle.

God put a crook in your arm to hook into another fellow's and bring him to church.

A holy life will produce the deepest impression. Lighthouses blow no horns; they only shine.— D. L. MOODY

The Lord did not say, "Let your light so twinkle" but "Let it shine."

There are too many Arctic River Christians—frozen at the mouth.

We do not stand in the world bearing witness to Christ, but we do stand in Christ and bear witness to the world.—GORDON

As Christians must account for every idle word, so we likewise must account for every idle silence.

If Christians praised God more the world would doubt Him less.—CHARLES JEFFERSON

The serene silent beauty of a holy life is the most powerful influence in the world, next to the might of God.—PASCAL

Truth is not only violated by falsehood; it may be equally outraged by silence.—AMIEL

WILLINGNESS

God never asks about our ability or our inability but our availability.

WORK

I must lose myself in action lest I wither in despair.

An hour's industry will do more to produce cheerfulness, suppress evil humor and retrieve your affairs than a month's moaning.—BENJAMIN FRANKLIN

The highest reward for man's toil is not what he gets for it, but what he becomes by it.—JOHN RUSKIN

It is two per cent genius and ninty-eight per cent honest effort that brings about success in any line of work.—THOMAS A. EDISON

The dictionary is the only place you can find SUCCESS before WORK.

Get your happiness out of your work or you will never know what happiness is.

You will never be saved by works, but let us tell you most solemnly that you will never be saved without works.—THEODORE L. CUYLER

If people knew how hard I have had to work to gain my mastery, it would not seem wonderful at all.—MICHELANGELO

If I have done any deed worthy of remembrance, that deed will be my monument. If not, no monument can preserve my memory.—AGESILAUS

People may doubt what you say but they will always believe what you do.

Great swelling words of beauty and eloquence are far less important than one tiny act of kindness.

A mule can't kick and pull at the same time, neither can a church member.

The fellow who pulls the oars seldom has time to rock the boat.

Work is the sole palliative for sorrow, the one way to escape worry, the only method of keeping a sound body and mind.—MRS. WALTER FERGUSON

WORSHIP

The sun meets not the springing bud that stretches toward it with half the certainty as God, the source of all good, communicates Himself to the soul that longs to partake of Him.—EVELYN UNDERHILL

117

In the secret place of my heart there is a little door through which, if I open and enter, I am in the Presence of God.—JOSEPH FORT NEWTON

Satan doesn't care what we worship, as long as we don't worship God.—D. L. MOODY

Women will remain the weaker sex just as long as they are smarter.

It is a wise wife who knows when to overlook and when to oversee.—ANNA HERBERT

Woman was made from Adam's side that she might walk beside him, not from his foot that he should step on her.—HAROLD LINDSELL

If you would change a woman's mind, begin by agreeing with her.

Men ought to be mighty good to women for nature gave them the big end of the log to lift, and mighty little strength to do it with.—ABRAHAM LINCOLN

Women are wiser than men because they know less and understand more.—JAMES STEPHENS

She was not made out of his head to top him, nor out of his feet to be trampled upon by him, but out of his side to be equal to him, under his arm to be protected and near his heart to be loved.—MATTHEW HENRY

Men will always be what the women make them; if, therefore, you would have men great and virtuous, impress upon the minds of women what greatness and virtue are.—ROUSSEAU

A good wife and health are a man's best wealth.

WEARINESS

The Lord will forgive those who start late in life to serve Him, but He will not forgive those who quit early.

WAITING

Waiting is a common instrument of providential discipline for those to whom exceptional work has been assigned.

WAR

You can't win a war just as you can't win a fire. You can prevent it or put it out.—H. H. ARNOLD

War does not and never can prove which side is right, but only which side is the stronger.—JAMES HILTON

WORRY

You can't change the past but you can ruin a perfectly good present by worrying over the future.

Worry, like a rocking chair, will give you something to do, but it won't get you anywhere.

Today is the tomorrow we worried about yesterday.

Worry is interest paid on trouble before it is due.—DEAN INGE

Soaring eagles never worry about crossing rivers.

If you cannot help worrying, remember that worrying cannot help you either.

Worry does not empty the day of its troubles, but only of its strength.

The misfortunes hardest to bear are those which never came.—James Russell Lowell

WEALTH

The rich are not always Godly but the Godly are always rich.

Measure wealth by how much one would be worth if he lost all his money.

God is not only a present help in time of trouble, but a great help in keeping us out of trouble.

Grace, the grace of God, teaches us in the midst of life's greatest comforts to be willing to die, and in the midst of its greatest crosses to be willing to live.

Christians are like tea; their real strength is not drawn on until they get into hot water.

The quickest cure for grief is action.

Examine many of your troubles and you'll find your own name stamped on them as the manufacturer.

Pain is neither a blessing nor a curse. It is an opportunity.

You'll not understand pain until you understand that life is not a pursuit of happiness, a search for ease, but is a training for greatness.

Most heroes emerge not from halls of luxury but from dark paths of suffering and persecution.

I have never killed a man, but I have read many obituaries with a lot of pleasure.—CLARENCE DARROW

It is not until a man gets nearly to the top that the world is willing to give him a boost.

He is incapable of a truly good action who has no pleasure in praising good actions in others.

The refusal of praise is only the wish to be praised twice.

Better associate with a cheerful idiot than a sour-pickle sage.

Only sin can rid a Christian of his joy.

God loves a cheerful doer as well as a cheerful giver.

Today is the beginning of the rest of your entire life.

Hope for the best, get ready for the worst; take cheerfully what God chooses to send.

Some people want a religion that makes them feel respectable without requiring them to be.

Merely sharing another's burden is noble. To share it cheerfully is sublime.

If good people learned to be agreeable it would win many to the good cause.

Life asks no questions that faith cannot answer.

Some people devote all of their religion to going to church.

The church is not a refrigerator for perishable piety but a dynamo for charging men.

Religious differences are not nearly so disastrous as religious indifference.

The church influences the world only when she has nothing to do with the world.

At church the early bird gets the back seat.

The church is not a circle of chasity but an outpost for outcasts.

Conceited men are like toy balloons: a pin prick and there is nothing left of them.

It's funny how we deem men clever and remarkable because they think as we do.

Feeding conceit into a vacuum results in an affliction of the upper part of the skull known as "big-head-edness."

Some conceited people are so busy talking about themselves that they have no time to talk about others.

The only exercise some people get is throwing bouquets at themselves.

Some men are so conceited that they send telegrams of congratulations to their mothers for having given them birth.

How strange that some who are deaf to counsel are so susceptible to flattery!

The devil convicts us of other people's sins. The Holy Spirit convicts us of our own.

He who makes God first will find God with him at the last.

An unsatisfied life results from an unsurrendered will.

We either lay self aside or God lays us aside.

The secrets of the Lord are revealed only to those who keep no secrets from Him.

It's easier to build temples than to be temples of the Holy Spirit.

Judge great men by the courtesy they show toward little men.

To pleasantly tolerate bad manners means you have good manners.

A polite man in the modern sense always offers his seat to a woman when he leave a bus, streetcar or crowded restaurant.

We reveal ourselves by what we do when we have nothing to do.

The lazier a man is the more he intends to do tomorrow.

Some fellows are always behind time until it's time to quit.

Almost without exception, he who has put faith out of his heart has first put obedience out of his life.

God has no larger field for the man who is not faithfully doing his work where he is.

Any coward can praise Christ, but it takes a man of courage to follow Him.

For most of us it is not that our aim is too high and we miss it, but that it is too low and we reach it.

It takes more courage to face ridicule than a cannon.

A person down in the mouth is never up on his toes.

Consider the postage stamp. Its usefulness lies in its ability to stick to one thing until it gets there.

It's better to pardon too much rather than condemn too much.

It's usually easier to forgive an enemy than a friend.

He who cannot forgive others, breaks the bridge over which he himself must pass.

He who ceases to be your friend never was a good one.

Promises may get friends, but it is performance that keeps them.

Have no friends you dare not bring home.

Some friends remain faithful to us in misfortune, but only the loftiest will remain after our errors and sins have come to light.

When you give some one a cup of milk, don't skim it.

A man does not own his wealth as much as he owes it.

Pretending to be rich keeps many people poor.

The love of money for right use is the root of much good.

Only the crazy give alms to the lazy.

The sun never boasts of its brightness and an honest man need not boast about his honesty.

Straightforward and simple integrity baffles a man full of duplicity and deceit.

Branches bearing the most fruit hang the lowest.

He is truly a humble man who feels no pride when people praise him for his humility.

Children are the only people wise enough to enjoy today without regretting yesterday or fearing tomorrow.

You must bring up your children is such a way that someone else likes them beside yourself.

Free men are never equal, and equal men are never free.

It's true; we are created equal with one area excepted: genius vs. morons.

Deliberate much before you say or do anything, for it will not be in your power to recall what is said or done.—EPICTETUS

Learning to cover up an aching heart, to smile when you would weep, is what everyone must learn if he would live the masterful life.

SOME BLESS THEIR CROSS

Two men on crosses hung
And each man sought release,
One sought release from nails,
The other, inner peace.
One sought escape from shame,
The other turned to Christ;
One asked to be set free,
One begged for Paradise.
One cursed his cross and died—
His life a tragic story;
The other used his cross
To catapult to glory.
Today we each have crosses
That last while life endures;
Some bless their cross, some curse.
What have you done with yours?

History shows that Christ on the cross has been more
potent than anything else in arousing a compas-
sion for suffering and indignation at injustice.—
FOAKES-JACKSON

CAUGHT IN A BINDER

I have to eat with me;
I have to sleep with me;
I have to work with me;
What then ought I to be?
Should I ignore myself?
Or try escaping self?
But I'm stuck with myself;
What choices then are left?
Lord, I'm caught in a binder
And I need no reminder.
To friends I must be kinder,
And to their faults much blinder.

KILLING CHILDHOOD DREAMS

May I not be accused
Of planned or unplanned scheming
To crush my children's dreams
When they're caught up with dreaming.
For there's no viler deed
Parents ever do
Than killing childhood dreams,
Saying they can't come true.
Lord, let me with my children
And for the sake of truth
Encourage dreaming dreams
As I dreamed in my youth.

Many owe the grandeur of their lives to their many
difficulties.

FAITH TO MOVE A HILL

Great faith to move a mountain
Would surely give a thrill,
But I'd be glad to have
A faith to move some hills.
For hills have slowed me down,
And things I cannot master;
And faith must move them surely
If I move forward faster.
Lord, let saints move their mountains!
The one thing that I'm needing
Is faith to deal with hills
That keeps me from succeeding.

The beginning of anxiety is the end of faith and the
beginning of true faith is the end of anxiety.—
GEORGE MUELLER

WHEN CHILDREN PRAY

When little children kneel to pray
I think God is not far away,
And softest prayers their lips intone
I think reach up to heaven's throne.
And blest are parents day by day
Who teach their children how to pray,
For children's prayers are always heard
When offered up in children's words.
And every little child that prays
Redeems the earth in countless ways,
For children, kneeling, lisping prayers
Is of all gifts our nation shares,
The surest hope, the promise grand
That God will bless and spare this land.

TO POISON A CHILD

What if I with some poison
Defiled my children's food?
The courts would brand me *criminal*—
Unfit to be excused.
Yet I with impure thoughts
Can poison my child's mind,
And go on unsuspected
Of vilest deed unkind.
Yet poisoning children's food,
Or water that he's drinking,
Is certainly no more dangerous
Than poisoning children's thinking.